SPECIAL EDUCATION SERIES
Peter Knoblock, Editor

Achieving the Complete School: Strategies for Effective Mainstreaming
Douglas Biklen
with Robert Bogdan, Dianne L. Ferguson,
Stanford J. Searl, Jr., and Steven J. Taylor

Classic Readings in Autism
Anne M. Donnellan, Editor

Achieving
THE COMPLETE SCHOOL
Strategies for Effective Mainstreaming

Douglas Biklen
with
Robert Bogdan
Dianne L. Ferguson
Stanford J. Searl, Jr.
Steven J. Taylor

Foreword by Burton Blatt

TEACHERS COLLEGE PRESS

Teachers College, Columbia University
New York and London

Published by Teachers College Press, 1234 Amsterdam Avenue,
New York, N.Y. 10027

Library of Congress Cataloging in Publication Data

Biklen, Douglas.
  Achieving the complete school.

  (Special education series)
  Bibliography: p.
  Includes index.
    1. Handicapped children—Education—United States—
Addresses, essays, lectures. 2. Mainstreaming in educa-
tion—United States—Addresses, essays, lectures.
I. Title. II. Series: Special education series (New
York, N.Y.)
LC4031.B47 1985   371.9'046   84-26911

ISBN 0-8077-2772-5 (paperback)
ISBN 0-8077-2773-3 (cloth)

Manufactured in the United States of America
98 97 96 95 94 93   9 8 7 6

Contents

Foreword

"Is mainstreaming a good idea?" My colleagues at Syracuse University begin this intriguing work with that question, but they quickly inform us that it's the *wrong* question. And of course, they're right. A more interesting question is always about the meaning of a term—whether it's mainstreaming, religion, marriage, you name it. Is marriage a good idea? If we look at the divorce rates, if we want to worry ourselves about the throngs of the unhappily married, then we must conclude that marriage is a bad idea. And if we remember the Crusades, or others who have failed or died in the name of God, then not only religion but even God would be a bad idea.

So, what's a right question? How do things work? Better, why do some things turn out poorly? Still better, how do we make our ideas work well? Even if most marriages are sour, the trick isn't to abolish marriage but to find out what's wrong, learn how to fix bad marriages—possibly even learn how to prevent bad marriages. There's no doubt that the world would be lost for the lack of good ideas. And there's no doubt that the world has been improved if not saved by those with the resolve to implement good ideas. But on a more modest level, one can harbor the notion that the world is made better by those who seek to learn how things work—who are as interested in solving puzzles as others are in perpetrating dilemmas.

This book truly illuminates an issue in American education that virtually everyone in the field professes to know something about and that virtually no one knows enough about. What is the nature of integration or, if that's your preference, mainstreaming? Is it simply placing disabled children in regular classes? If it is, some call that dumping. Others have even nastier names for it. At one time, the most intelligent, the most sophisticated, the most humanitarian leaders in our field were segregators. If that's so, could they have been so wrong—and could almost everyone today be right about what children and their teachers need and want? Why today do we claim that nothing good can happen for disabled children in segregated settings, and not too many years ago our lineal if not ideological ancestors claimed that nothing good happened for disabled children in integrated settings?

You are in for a fine experience. If you are interested in disabled children, or in all children, you'll have the opportunity here to ponder the issue of equity in a society bent on excellence. If you're not one of those people who sit on their hands while the parade is passing, you'll find here ways people can think about a problem to turn it to the advantage of not only the person with the problem but also to the enrichment of the larger society. It isn't only that integration is good for the handicapped but also that it's necessary for *all* people. That is the prepotent lesson in this absorbing book. Normalization is not only for handicapped people. By definition, it can't be only for handicapped people. It must be imbedded in each of us—in each of you, in me. Working with people who have disabilities is important not only for them, not only for those who do the work, but if it's to mean anything it will be important to everyone. The question always comes back to, How do we maximize variance? How can our lives be enlarged by living, by working, by associating with people of all colors, all backgrounds, all ages, all interests? The book's thesis is that not only is integration successful, but we too are successful, if we are committed to it.

I wish that people out of the field of special education, out of the field of mental health, those not professionally or personally concerned with mental retardation, mental illness, blindness, deafness, autism, or physical handicaps, would read this book. In it there is a lesson for everyone—that all people are valuable, and that our lives are enriched and fulfilled as we live by that wisdom. Good work, my friends Doug Biklen, Bob Bogdan, Dianne Ferguson, Stan Searl, and Steve Taylor. Your book can teach us about almost everything that's obvious about human relationships, and about almost everything that's neglected. Good work. Good deed.

BURTON BLATT

Preface

The term *mainstreaming* has become so common to the field of education in recent years that nearly everyone has at least a vague sense about what it means. Some people have very definite feelings about mainstreaming. Some like it. Some hate it. But others are not sure about it.

Throughout this book we use the terms *mainstreaming* and *integration* interchangeably. Mainstreaming is the more popular word for integrating students with disabilities into regular classes and/or into regular schools (i.e., self-contained classes in regular schools). We use mainstreaming to mean the integration of disabled and nondisabled students in regular schools. This may occur in regular classes, in the lunchroom, in hallways, in particular subjects, in school assemblies, and in extracurricular activities.

Achieving the Complete School is based on two extensive studies of mainstreaming. One study is of successful mainstreaming programs in public schools in one metropolitan area. Under a grant from the National Institute of Education, we did in-depth observational case studies of twenty-five mainstreaming programs in a typical American city and its surrounding school districts. We asked hundreds of teachers, administrators, and parents to nominate mainstreaming programs they considered successful. We then chose the twenty-five programs that received the most nominations and were representative of urban, suburban, and rural districts, of the range of types of disabilities, and of preschool, elementary, and secondary levels. The other study was of programs throughout the country that have a reputation for having promising ways of serving the most severely and multiply disabled students. Here, we polled experts in universities, special education administrators, and the network of special education regional resource centers nationally for their nominations of programs that they felt displayed "promising practices" for schools. Then we visited twenty such programs and documented our findings. Our focus was on specific strategies that people employ to promote successful integration.

In this book we discuss positive examples and positive results, as well as instances where integration has literally failed, or at least not lived up to our expectations or apparently to those of the people involved in trying to carry it out or benefit from it. Inasmuch as the book is a "how-to" guide on integration, we have attempted to speak to those who would like to make integration work. But we also hope that people who may find mainstreaming perplexing or even exasperating will find this book useful.

We do not take the position that integration happens naturally, without planning, support, or other special consideration. Nor do we adhere to the notion that integration always succeeds in schools where people want it to work. Yet it can work. In this book, we address the questions, When does it work, why, and how?

Achieving the Complete School includes principles and strategies that have been tried and proven effective, virtually all of which could be employed in almost any public school or school district immediately, at little or no additional expense. The book includes brief as well as extended case examples to illustrate the complexities of integration and the relationship of integration to the culture of schools and the myriad other critical issues that swirl in and around schools.

Each aspect of the book, the principles, the practices, and the case vignettes, is based on the experiences of scores of administrators, teachers, and parents. And each element is based on the two research projects that were carried out simultaneously over three years. The data upon which we have based the book are largely empirical, by which we mean observational and descriptive. All unreferenced passages are drawn from the observational studies. Two examples (Mrs. O'Day and Mrs. Lake in chapter three) are composites built upon observations of more than one classroom and teacher, a strategy of presentation used to communicate a number of findings quickly. Unless otherwise indicated, we have used fictitious names in all the observational passages. The authors and teams of researchers spent hundreds of hours in schools and classrooms observing, recording conversations, conducting interviews, talking to parents and administrators, finding out what students had to say about their education, and attempting to build an understanding of this phenomenon that we refer to variously as mainstreaming and integration. Our goal was not to prove that one factor has more or less influence than another in making integration work, but rather to understand the overall phenomenon and, to the extent possible, the interaction of factors. We wanted to get a sense of what integration means to the different groups involved in it. We wanted to interpret mainstreaming's place in education.

The method of our research might be called ethnography, participant observation, the case method, or naturalistic research. We have referred to it simply as qualitative research, though each of the other terms applies in whole or in part to what we did.

Each chapter, except for the first and last ones, addresses the particular role of a different group, namely district special education administrators, school building principals, teachers, and parents. We have written the book for each of these groups as well as for others like ourselves who study such phenomena as mainstreaming. The chapter on special education directors addresses primarily this group because these are the district level administrators who most often play a central role in implementing integration policies. However, we hasten to admit that any district administrator, whether a superintendent, pupil personnel director, supervisor of curriculum, or other manager, can use the principles and strategies in this chapter. Similarly, the teacher chapter is as useful for parents, principals, and district special education directors as for teachers. In fact, the same can be said for each chapter. Simply stated, each group becomes more effective when it understands the basic nature of the other groups' roles.

Mainstreaming of students with disabilities in regular public schools has posed a challenge for schools. But, mainstreaming has been no more of a test to schools than other similar efforts to introduce change. In many ways, it was been much like racial integration, open education, and sex education. It is a new phenomenon. It challenges old ways of doing things. It raises eyebrows, even hackles. It tends to become a lightning rod for people's emotions about schools in general.

The conventional way people have regarded mainstreaming is as a special activity best understood and implemented by specialists, or special educators. Thus many school district administrators, superintendents, as well as pupil personnel officers and others have regarded mainstreaming as the province of these special educators, in much the same way that matters of racial equality are commonly thought to be the special concern of affirmative action officers, minority specialists, or minority faculty. Yet it has almost never been completely possible to contain the effects of such important matters. Once specialists begin to introduce new programs—for example, to place students with disabilities in regular schools—

this automatically affects school life. At this point, and at many other decision points, the "let's-leave-it-to-specialists" mind-set gives way to the political decision-making process. Therein lies one of the dilemmas posed by mainstreaming. On the one hand, it might be convenient to leave it to the experts. On the other, the decision to foster integration, and each subsequent decision related to it, is basically a decision founded on values and priorities.

   In this book we examine not only technical special education/regular education issues, such as principles for curriculum planning, but also basic aspects of organization and change that make integration work. While we include practical strategies related to curricula and program models, unlike virtually every other book about mainstreaming, this is not a book on curriculum modification. But neither is it primarily a discourse on ideology or philosophy. We point out and discuss a few specialized concepts such as functional programming, developmental models, and community-referenced instruction, but we devote more energy and space to basic educational and organizational methods that will promote integration. The essence of the book is the experience and lessons to be learned from integration as we have observed them in America's schools.

Acknowledgments

While we take full responsibility for the ideas and suggestions that comprise this book, we are indebted to many for their contributions. We wish to thank the researchers on both studies whose case studies and site-visit reports helped provide data for this book: Ellen Barnes, Carol Berrigan, Judy Kugelmass, Sandra Mlinarcik, Philip Ferguson, Michele Sokoloff, Mary Cantey, Sue Lesure, Susanne Fitzgerald, Stephani Bruni, Ann Pia, Deborah Olson, Daniel Seklecki, Edward Burke, and Suzanne Gilmour. We owe special thanks to Rosemary Alibrandi who helped type numerous drafts, who kept track of voluminous notes and dozens of case studies, and who managed the budgets for both research projects. To the advisory board of the NIE-funded mainstreaming project for their ever practical and insightful commentaries on our presentations of data and interpretations we express our appreciation. We extend our gratitude to Peter Knoblock, who gave us strong encouragement in the final stage of this project and helped us decide on revisions. Our thanks to Alison Ford, Michael Steer, Mary Johnson, Allen Crocker, Daniel Sage, and Gerald Grant for their careful, substantive, and invaluable criticisms of the penultimate draft. Finally, Burton Blatt's comments on the manuscript helped immensely. We are grateful to him for these comments and for those he offered in his Foreword to this book.

Achieving
THE COMPLETE SCHOOL
Strategies for Effective Mainstreaming

1

Getting Started

DOUGLAS BIKLEN

Asking the question, "Is mainstreaming a good idea?" is a bit like asking, "Is Tuesday a good idea?" Both are wrong questions. It's not so much whether mainstreaming and Tuesday are good ideas as what we make of them. In the past three years we have visited more than one hundred schools across America. In more than two dozen we have observed school life and, particularly, mainstreaming intensively. As we could easily have predicted, we have seen good and bad mainstreaming. Just as we can look back on all the Tuesdays in our lives and say, "There have been good ones and bad ones," we can also see that mainstreaming can succeed, fail, or just muddle along. Therefore, to ask, "Does it work?" is also to ask the wrong question.

IS MAINSTREAMING A GOOD IDEA?

For obvious reasons, it is hard to escape this "wrong question." Skeptics of mainstreaming, as well as many like ourselves who are sympathetic to it, want some "evidence" upon which to base their beliefs. "Will handicapped students learn better if integrated?" "Will nondisabled students develop better attitudes about their disabled peers if they rub shoulders with them?" Or is mainstreaming just a fad? Will "normal" students lose ground because more of the teacher's time will be devoted to the special students? In other words, what are the facts about mainstreaming? Is there some scientific evidence that mainstreaming makes good sense educationally and socially?

1

Unfortunately, science cannot offer a positive or negative answer on mainstreaming. An analogy may make the point clearer. At the time of the American Civil War, should Abraham Lincoln have asked to see the scientific evidence on the benefits of ending slavery? Should he have consulted "the experts," perhaps a sociologist, an economist, a political scientist? Of course not. True, Lincoln made compromises and delayed before issuing the Emancipation Proclamation; he believed the immorality of slavery needed to be weighed against other values (e.g., keeping the nation united), but he never lost sight of the basis upon which slavery should be evaluated.

Slavery is not now and was not then an issue for science. It is a moral issue. But, just for a moment, suppose that an economist had been able to demonstrate that blacks would suffer economically, as would the entire South, from emancipation. Would that justify keeping slavery? And suppose a political scientist had argued that blacks had no experience with democracy, they were not ready for it. Would that have justified extending slavery? Or imagine that a sociologist could have advised Lincoln against abolishing slavery on the grounds that it would destroy the basic social structure of southern plantations, towns, and cities. From a racist perspective, all of these arguments might have seemed "true." But could they really justify slavery? Of course not. Slavery has no justification.

Take another example, this time from education. We have ample evidence that it is difficult to educate autistic students, particularly those with severe autism. Students who do not read, who communicate little if at all verbally, who have problems in coordinating their hands and feet, who sometimes (even often) behave in seemingly bizarre ways (i.e., screaming, self-stimulatory behavior), and who frequently have very short attention spans try the talents of even very skilled teachers. Some experts have suggested that the difficulty of teaching such students through traditional methods, and the fact that they abuse themselves regularly, justify "treating" them with aversive conditioning such as, for example, isolating them in locked rooms for short periods of time or even giving them electric shocks with cattle prods. Those who advocate shocks and isolation do so out of their conviction that "nothing else works" or that "nothing works as well." Of course others, ourselves included, have amassed incontrovertible evidence that even the so-called most difficult can benefit from educational strategies that do not include aversive conditioning. But even more important, we believe that, irrespective of "the evidence," certain practices have no place in education. Using shocks, however "safe" or "effective," is tantamount to assault and battery. It offends our sensibilities and dehumanizes those upon whom it is used. And so we reject such practices outright. For some things we need no evidence. The practice itself is simply not acceptable.

We approach the topic of mainstreaming similarly. The question of whether or not to promote mainstreaming is not essentially a question for science. It is a moral question. It is a goal, indeed a value, we decide to pursue or reject on the basis of what we want our society to look like.

WHAT DOES MAINSTREAMING MEAN?

The term *mainstreaming* defies simple definition. For some people it is a code word for "dumping." To these people, it means placing students with disabilities into regular classes and providing no support services, no teacher preparation, and no special assistance to nondisabled students on how to relate to their disabled peers. Others say mainstreaming means carefully integrating students with disabilities into regular schools and classes with the appropriate support services and planning. Our two studies suggest that mainstreaming means different things to different people and takes many forms. These forms are described later in this chapter in the section "Will the Real Mainstreaming Please Stand Up?"

In this section, we examine what mainstreaming means. What does it mean to principals? What does it mean to teachers? What does it mean to parents? What does it mean for education in America? In other words, we believe that the only way to understand mainstreaming, to define it for ourselves, is to understand the meaning that people attach to it. And it may mean different things to different people, depending on such factors as their roles (for example whether the person is a principal or parent), their specific encounters with it, and their attitudes about disabilities.

For some people mainstreaming means complying with the law, either because they want to or feel they must. A study parallel to our own (Brightman and Sullivan, 1980) found that parents regard lawsuits and the federal special education law, the Right to Education for All Handicapped Children Act (Public Law 94-142, 1975), as something that empowers them to demand equal access to schooling for their children. Thus, many parents regard mainstreaming as a principal right, as a symbol

of their children's worthiness. From others, particularly from administrators charged with implementing the law, we have heard, alternately,
"it's the law, we are obligated to mainstream students wherever appropriate," or "the law gives us the wedge we need to break down the age-
old barriers to handicapped students and to get them out of privately
operated handicapped centers, institutions, and school basements into the
mainstream of school life where they belong."

October 7, 1971, marked a watershed victory for children with disabilities. From that day, when a decision was handed down in the case
formally titled *The Pennsylvania Association for Retarded Citizens v. the
Commonwealth of Pennsylvania (PARC v. Penn,* 1971; see also, Dybwad,
1980), the right of handicapped children to education became part of
most American educators' consciousness. For parents of students with
disabilities, PARC vindicated years of struggle against the social injustice
of school exclusion. The PARC case, like more than one hundred subsequent cases styled after it, embodied at least five claims that the court
endorsed: (1) that students with disabilities, in this case retarded students,
had systematically, and at great individual and social cost, been denied
a public education; (2) that all students could benefit from an education
(testimony of Blatt and Goldberg, reported in Lippman and Goldberg,
1973); (3) that under the constitutional right of equal protection and various state claims, all students were entitled to a free appropriate education
at public expense; (4) that parents had a right to due process by which
they might question particular classification and placement decisions for
their children; and (5) that students with disabilities were entitled to receive
their education in the least restrictive environment possible.

Each of the five findings stirred controversy. How much would all
this cost? Would the nature of public schools change overnight? Who
would teach those students who heretofore had not been admitted to
school? But, in fact, all but one of the provisions was straightforward
and easily interpreted into practice, albeit sometimes hesitantly. After all,
evidence in the case proved that there had been a long tradition of non-
service for the plaintiffs (see Task Force, 1969, and Children's Defense
Fund, 1974, for evidence of the exclusion problem nationally). Further,
nationally renowned educational experts had stated unequivocally that all
children were educable. It followed that all children were entitled to an
education. Anything less would violate standards of equality set forth in
the U.S. Constitution. In view of the problems encountered by parents
in securing educational programs, it made good sense for the courts to

mandate parental due process rights with respect to classification and placement. But the final principle, the notion that each student was entitled to an education in "the least restrictive environment" possible, began a debate that is far from over (Public Law 94–142, 1975). It is the mainstreaming debate. The court-approved consent decree read:

> It is the Commonwealth's obligation to place each mentally retarded child in a free, public program of education and training appropriate to the child's capacity, within the context of the general educational policy that, among the alternative programs of education and training required by statute to be available, placement in a regular public school is preferable to placement in a special public school class and placement in a public school class is preferable to placement in any other type of program of education and training. (*PARC v. Penn*, 1971)

Did this mean that all children, irrespective of the severity of their disabilities, would be mainstreamed? Did it mean that institutions as well as private and public segregated schools for disabled children only would go out of business? How should parents and educators interpret the concept? What criteria should they use?

Congress did not settle the controversy by legislating the "least restrictive" principle nationally. Public Law 94-142 (1975) does not define the words "least restrictive environment," but the concept is implied:

> To the maximum extent appropriate, handicapped children, including children in public or private institutions or other care facilities, are educated with children who are not handicapped, and that special classes, separate schooling, or other removal of handicapped children from the regular educational environment occurs only when the nature or severity of the handicap is such that education in regular classes with the use of supplementary aids and services cannot be achieved satisfactorily. (20 U.S.C. 1412[5] [B])

All this means that mainstreaming has a legal basis but one that calls on practitioners, namely principals, teachers, and parents, to define it in practical terms. It is up to the schools to demonstrate what shape mainstreaming will take in future years.

"As Normal as Possible"

The word *mainstreaming* was coined in America. The concept received its first serious airing in 1962 when a special education professor, Maynard Reynolds (1962), called for "a continuum of placements for children with handicaps." There was a sense that segregation, particularly in the forms of separate classes, separate schools, and segregated institutions, had been overdone and was largely unnecessary, even unjustifiable (Dunn, 1968; Blatt, 1969). Yet, three years before Reynolds published his article on integration, a related concept known as "Normalization" was taking shape in Scandinavia. Many people in America, including many whom we met in the course of our two studies, now regard mainstreaming as the educational equivalent of normalization.

Bank-Mikkelsen, a Dane, coined the term *normalization* in 1959. With the word *normalization* he characterized the policy of permitting people with disabilities opportunities to live in as normal a fashion as possible. America learned about the concept largely through the work of another Scandinavian, Bengt Nirje (Kugel and Wolfensberger, 1969). Wolfensberger has since extended the term's application to other disability groups. Nirje defined normalization as "making available to the mentally retarded patterns and conditions of everyday life which are as close as possible to the norms and patterns of the mainstream of society." More recently, Wolfensberger (1983) has suggested that the term *social role valorization* better captures the essence of this process than does normalization.

One of Nirje's favorite examples, to illustrate the concept of normalization, grew out of a conference held in Scandinavia while he was the executive director of the Swedish Association for Retarded Children. At the conference, retarded people were asked to make requests for policy changes that might affect their lives. Their requests were consistent with the normalization principle. People asked not to be given special preference in receiving housing referrals (there were housing shortages in Sweden). The retarded people also said that when taken into town they preferred not to be taken in large groups but rather to go in groups of two or three. And they asked that as adults they not be sent to special camps for the retarded only, but that they be given opportunities to take their vacations in the standard vacation resorts of Europe as nonretarded people do.

It was just a short step for American educators and disability rights advocates to apply the principle of normalization to education. At one school, we observed normalization in practice. The following account was provided by one of our field researchers:

It is obvious that the teachers at this school try to measure success with mainstreaming in terms of what professionals in the field call "normalization."

Take, for example, Jamie. As one of the staff noted, Jamie entered the school
with the same facial expressions which are rather typical for profoundly mentally retarded persons. "He looked like a child who would usually be put in a
segregated class. His mouth was open; his head would hang; his eyes would
be down or wandering. But now, he really looks in people's eyes a lot. He's
focusing." When the class celebrated Jamie's birthday, he smiled when a
classmate said "Happy Birthday." And he clapped his hands when the teacher
congratulated him. While at the school he became nearly flawless in learning
to use the toilet. All of these gains in appearance in basic living skills contrib-
uted to the goal of normalization. Interestingly, the search for ways to pursue
what seemed like an integration imperative were ongoing. One day, one of
the teachers suggested that the process of Jamie getting off the bus could be
improved:

Sally: Don't you think that we could have him get his boots off himself and
      also maybe we could leave that harness that he wears on the bus.
Margaret: Yes, I think that would be a good idea. Why don't we try and
      see if we can leave the harness and then the other kids won't ques-
      tion him about it. (*Everyone nodded.*)
Jim: I was visiting a school the other day and this autistic kid had his har-
      ness on all day long and the teachers thought there was nothing
      wrong with leaving the harness on all day. (*Several of the teachers
      in the meeting groaned and one said, "Oh God," as if to say "how
      could they care so little about normalization."*)
Sally: Maybe he should unhook it himself.

Later, we observed how the teachers helped Jamie become more a part of
the class by having him participate in class activities and routines which
approximated the norm set by nondisabled students (ages 5–7). At the beginning of each day, all the children in the class sit around in a circle. The
teacher asks one of the children to tell what month it is. Another tells the day
of the month. And still another the day of the week. Then each child is asked
to share an experience or wish. This is called "news of the day." The teacher
writes down the news. For Jamie, who does not talk, the teachers learned
from the group home staff or from his parents what he has done over the
weekend. This has been volunteered by the teacher and written down with the
other children's comments. When school began, Jamie did not know how to
go up to the chart, a teacher had to help him each step of the way. But one
day he learned how.

There was a class meeting going on and Jamie was part of the meeting,
but with teacher restraint, having his back rubbed and having physical cues,
being helped back down to his chair, and having his head stroked so that he
would remain in his chair during the class meeting. Heidi, the lead teacher,

asked Jamie to come up and check off his name. He can do that. When he crossed the room, he walked across the circle to the pad that Heidi was holding and she gave him a magic marker so he could make a mark on the paper next to his name. As he walked across the circle, his arms and legs were going in different directions and he was jumping around and we were kind of wondering if he was actually going to make it or if he was going to bolt out of the circle. At that point in the year, if Jamie were going to bolt out of the circle, he would probably run around and knock things down. He was easily excitable. I watched one of the children in the class just looking and grinning at Jamie and she exclaimed "Look at Jamie, he is really feeling good today." Instead of laughing or saying "what is he doing" or being shocked by his arms and legs and playing with his hair, the kids watched with interest. He was really an active body crossing that circle. And he made it. He checked off his name.

It Scorns Limits, It Covets Potential

Quite some time ago, I asked a college student to interview teachers about their goals for their students. This student, the interviewer, queried both regular class teachers and special education teachers. This was before the passage of Public Law 94-142 and before the recent emphasis in American schools on providing equal opportunity for students with disabilities. On the whole, the regular and special class teachers responded differently. Most regular class teachers said they strived to prepare their students for going out in the world and making their mark. They spoke of their students as future leaders, as people who would make a difference. The special class teachers, on the other hand, spoke of adjustment and of finding happiness. Most expressed their goal as "helping the students learn how to cope with community life."

In each of our studies of integration we have uncovered a new way of thinking about students with disabilities. Teachers, both regular and special, continue to speak of adjustment to community life as an important goal for disabled students, but they also mention some more ambitious goals. They speak of helping students become as independent as possible, of competing for typical jobs, of overcoming the impediment of their disabilities, of achieving their true potential.

This notion of potential, of overcoming limits, surfaces again and again as an important justification for mainstreaming. It comes up, for example, in regard to labeling.

Disability is a personal quality or attribute. Like hair color, body height, even color, weight, and personality, this particular attribute need not become the dominant quality by which people are identified. Yet, it often plays just such a dominant role. Disability, like certain other personal qualities (for example, race, place of birth, political allegiance) may be so negatively valued that to have a disability means being defined by that single attribute and, thus, devalued as a person. We call that phenomenon, the negative valuation by reason of an attribute, stigma (Goffman, 1963). Another way to think about it is to regard it as an imposition of limits, a denial of individuality and of individual potential.

No natural law dictates that society must always stigmatize people who possess certain attributes. Indeed, we know, from cross-cultural studies (e.g., Eaton and Weil, 1955) as well as from other social research (Goffman, 1963) that societies and individuals manufacture stigma. It is learned behavior. It can be changed. More importantly, research suggests that the single most effective way of combating stigma is through planned personal interaction of those who traditionally give stigma and those who are its recipients (Yuker, 1965). A leading researcher on interactional behavior between disabled and nondisabled persons had this to say about integration:

> The legislation that will make disabled people visible—in schools, in buses, in apartment buildings—will bring some good with more contact. One thing my research tells me is that frequency of contact improves one's comfort with handicapped people. (Kleck in Kleinfeld, 1979)

A recent study of children's attitudes toward mental retardation suggests that young, school-age children generally base their impressions and opinions about "the mentally retarded" on their knowledge of *one* retarded person whom they know or have met (Brightman, 1977). Clearly, a single experience will more likely produce stereotyped visions of what a disability is and of people with such an attribute. Only by bringing young people, disabled and nondisabled alike, together more frequently will we begin to rid ourselves of stereotypes. That is one of the principal benefits of integration (Voeltz 1980, 1982); it holds potential for students to learn about each other's humanness, uniqueness, and similarities. By contrast, continued segregation of disabled and nondisabled students can only help foster stereotypes.

Mainstreaming abandons limits and embraces potential in other ways as well. When we create integration programs we open up educational possibilities. How better to teach a student who is blind to get to the cafeteria than to practice with her seeing classmates, in the hubbub of the everyday school hallway? How better for a student with severe retardation to learn when to laugh, how to dress, and how to walk, than to observe his nondisabled peers? Certain recently developed curricula for successfully educating students with some of the most handicapping disabilities—for example, autism, severe and profound retardation, and multiple disabilities—actually *require* integrative schooling (Barnes, 1978; Knoblock, 1982; Guralnick, 1978; Guralnick, 1980; Vincent et al., 1980; Vincent and Broome, 1977; Brown et al., 1980; Brown et al., 1977; Brown et al., 1979a; Pumpian et al., 1979; Sailor et al., 1980; and Sternat et al., 1977). Throughout this book we offer scores of examples of how teachers and students are realizing the potential inherent in mainstreaming. These accounts, based on our researchers' reports, begin to tell the story about mainstreaming. For example, a parent of a child with autism who attends a unique integrated class in an elementary school comments as follows:

> My child can talk. And, that's one reason why he can. It's because of the other children. The typical children kept coming up to him and talking to him and demanding that he talk. They knew how to get an answer from him, and they wouldn't let him get away with a single-syllable response. Now I ask you, what teacher or teachers could do that for my son, much less for a whole class of kids with autism? That's just not realistic.

Or consider how the progress of a mainstreamed child with severe retardation is described by his elementary class teacher:

> In terms of his interacting with other kids, it has been aeons from where he started. He is noticing other kids. He's in the gym playing with the ball. He is playing with the other kids (chasing after the ball, bouncing it to them, catching it when it is thrown). In meetings he sits with the other kids, comes up and checks his name, and goes back to his seat. Today we had square dancing at the end of the day and he danced with Jacqueline. He looked at her when he was dancing.
>
> Kids tended to be frightened of Jamie. Now that is just totally gone. That has been amazing to watch. They don't really treat him like he is a little person or younger than they are. Jamie is just Jamie. I think they recognize he is a special person, that he is not the same as they are. They talk about the fact that he can't talk. Like one day Mario was watching Jamie sign at snack time and he asked how people who sign can talk on the telephone.

Of course, not all of the learning, the limit breaking, the striving for potential belongs solely to students with disabilities. Sarason and Doris (1979) have suggested that society has historically justified schools on two grounds: (1) to promote cognitive learning, and (2) to teach democracy. Predictably, they argue, schools have accomplished the former more effectively than the latter. Indeed, we know why. In order to teach democracy, schools must challenge dominant social attitudes about such things as race, sex stereotyping, and class differences. Many schools do not. Yet, we find evidence that, in at least some cases, mainstreaming has provided the impetus for schools to educate about democracy, equality, and civil rights. The beneficiaries of such efforts are the nondisabled as well as the disabled students.

The Twin Argument

If a child with a particular disability can benefit from educational programming in an integrated school setting, then one might argue that that child's developmental twins—i.e., all children with the same type and degree of disability, and similar behaviors associated with the disability—can also profit from integration. Therein lies the powerful logic of what legal advocates and educators have recently called the twin argument or the developmental twin argument.

Increasingly, as districts place special programs in regular schools, the argument that integration is not feasible loses its force. Developmental twins in integrated programs demonstrate the potential of integration for students still segregated. If we know integration can work—examples for children with every type of disability exist (e.g., Barnes, 1978; Sailor et al., 1980; Perske, 1979; Knoblock and Barnes, 1979; Scholl, 1978; Guralnick, 1980; Appoloni et al., 1977; Appoloni and Cooke, 1978; Bricker, 1978; Brown et al., 1979c; Northcutt, 1973)—then how can we still justify segregation? This increasingly worrisome question has motivated legal advocates to suggest that those who would call for more restrictive program sites (i.e., segregation) must demonstrate the relative advantage of that restriction:

> Under the statutes, any degree of segregation can be maintained only if it is necessary to the appropriate education of a child. There is no cognizable reason under the statutes—that is, no learning reason and no disability reason—for handicapped-only centers, certainly not on the scale they exist now. If a child

can come to a school at all, even to a self-contained class in a handicapped-
only center, he can come to a self-contained class in a normal school. Any
teaching technique that can be used in a self-contained class can be used in a
self-contained class located in a regular school building. There are few if any
legitimate teaching strategies which require the complete isolation of a child
from interaction with other children, and the few such strategies that there may
be apply to very few children and for very short periods of time. Such strategies
do not require massive segregated centers or massive institutions. (Gilhool and
Stutman, 1978)

In the absence of evidence that segregation yields superior benefits,
the mere existence of integrative programs for those children and youth
traditionally segregated (autistic children, severely disabled students) calls
into question continued segregation.

WILL THE REAL MAINSTREAMING PLEASE STAND UP?

In the previous section the question was asked, What does mainstreaming mean? In this section we ask, What does mainstreaming look
like in practice? What forms does it take? Will the real mainstreaming
please stand up?

The literature is filled with articles on the pros and cons of mainstreaming, its effects on students' psychological well-being, their academic development, and on each other's attitudes (National Education
Association, 1978; Cruickshank, 1977, Dybwad, 1980). But researchers
have paid little attention to the definitional problem. What is this thing
we call mainstreaming? We think it is an important question.

How should we talk about mainstreaming? Is it the same thing when
applied to deaf students as to blind students, to physically disabled students as to mentally retarded students, to students with speech impairments as to students with learning disabilities? Is it the same when applied
to young students as to older students? Does it mean placing mildly
disabled students in regular classes with little or no supports? Does it
mean providing special services in regular classes to selected students?
Does it mean locating classrooms of more severely disabled students in
regular public schools that also house classrooms for nondisabled students?

As with any social policy, particularly a new one, mainstreaming
takes many forms. It is not one thing. It cannot be neatly defined. Nowhere
in the federal law is mainstreaming defined. Thus, schools have been

relatively free to shape it in their own image or, more accurately, in their own images. Indeed, it takes all of the forms noted above. It can look different from one school or one district to another, depending on such factors as administrative structure and leadership, funding mechanisms and funding levels, staffing patterns, attitudes of individuals, types of disabilities, the social history of the school or community, parent involvement, skill levels of teachers, the style of providing related services such as speech therapy and physical therapy, diagnostic and assessment practices, and availability of special equipment.

Yet to say that mainstreaming defies simple definition is not to say that it defies definition altogether. And to say that mainstreaming does not take one form is not to say that it is anything and everything. Through our studies of schools, all types, ranging from preschools to high schools, from rural to suburban to urban, and in wealthy districts as well as poor ones, we found that integration takes several distinguishable forms or types. Of course, within each type of mainstreaming we found variation in particulars. We even found examples of the same type of mainstreaming that were opposite in quality, one seemingly successful and one relatively unsuccessful. In this section we describe the basic forms that mainstreaming takes. In the book as a whole we address more comprehensively the issue of quality and specifically how to achieve it.

Teacher Deals

In many schools mainstreaming comes about through informal grass-roots "deals." One teacher approaches another and says, "How about it; will you take Jane? I think she's ready. I think she can handle it." If the regular class teacher agrees, we have mainstreaming. Such deals rarely bring any kind of administrative support with them. The regular class teacher may receive some informal assistance from the special class teacher, usually on his or her own time, but again informally. In these situations, special class teachers rarely have "release time" from their regular responsibilities in their own classrooms to engage in such placement work. If they are lucky they have parent volunteers, student interns, or an aide to take over while they are helping the regular class teacher adjust.

Our observations reveal that special class teachers have two main criteria for determining who shall be mainstreamed. "Can the student conform to social expectations?" And, "Can the student make it academically, or at least with a slightly modified curriculum?" For example, if a regular class teacher perceives a child as "not making it," the problem may be disruptive behavior, a form of social differentness and a barrier for academic involvement. A teacher in this situation remarked to us: "She is working fine but the crying is like 85 percent. About three weeks ago she cried for the entire week. Her dog died. I mean, I'm supposed to teach this kid math?" Or the problem may be essentially academic but with a social implication. The teacher comments on how difficult it is for a student who performs at a different (i.e., lower) level than the other students:

We could look at it from a kid's point of view. I think April is on a second- or third-grade reading level. And I have sixth-grade kids. I teach these kids seventh-grade material and sixth-grade material; some high sixth, some low sixth, and I teach these kids fifth-grade material. Some kids get fourth-grade stuff. But how's it gonna look if she's all by herself doin' third-grade stuff? The kids know. It wouldn't be good psychologically.

In the world of "teacher deals," decisions about where a child should go, at least once a student has been initially placed, belong to the teachers involved. A "receiving" teacher puts it this way:

Not everybody is willing to do it. Even though the staff has been here so long, it's just been the last year that they have been willing to take the little handicapped kids in regular classes. I had to agree to take Jane in the first place. If I had said no, then that's it.

This model of mainstreaming not only requires regular teachers to express a sense of ownership for making mainstreaming happen, it gives teachers veto power over whether or not there will be mainstreaming of a particular student. But—and here is the great drawback to this model—at the same time, the teacher who does integrate a student often receives no measurable support from the school system or administration. To the extent that such a program is regarded as "successful" it can most often be attributed to a so-called super teacher.

In the following example, a child with a rather severe disability is mainstreamed. Those who observe this child and her classroom invariably point to the teacher and her skill at orchestrating mainstreaming as the single most important factor in the child's success.

Josey is by all definitions a severely handicapped child. Her mother says she has been "successfully mainstreamed." She told us what that means: "a handicapped child going to a public school, getting through everything all right."

Josey is five years old. She has cerebral palsy. She is very small and attractive. So far, she is nonverbal. Instead, she uses a language board to communicate. The board has pictures of people, objects and activities, and Bliss symbols, a system in which a symbol for a concept is paired with the printed word. The language board goes wherever Josey goes. It sits on a tray in front of her. Josey uses a light beam attached to her head to point to the large board. This is how she talks to all of the children in her group at one time.

Josey sits in a wheelchair or a stationary insert nearly all of the time. She has a difficult time controlling her arms, legs, and fingers. She participates at grade level in the learning parts of the kindergarten program.

Her physical therapist describes her schooling: "I was just thrilled at how Lynn integrated Josey into the mainstream of the group, the mainstream of the play activity. It was exciting for me to see because I've seen the opposite too. I have had children here that are 'mainstreamed, integrated' and what are they doing? An aide is pulling the child out of class and taking the child into a cubicle and doing her one-on-one. That's not mainstreaming. She is not working in the classroom setting while the other children are going about their duties and responsibilities. That is not mainstreaming. Josey was being mainstreamed. She had a chance to respond and participate at her level within her skill capacity with the other kids. They had to wait for her just as she would have to wait for another child that might be slower. It was a marvelous experience."

Such scenes are hard to replicate. They depend on a teacher's being motivated, well organized, able to find rewards inside the classroom, and willing to work long and hard.

We generally found teacher-initiated mainstreaming for severely as well as mildly disabled students only in the preschool and primary grades. At the secondary level, teacher deals involved only mildly disabled students.

With this form of mainstreaming it is common to find a hodgepodge of factors competing with each other, for and against integrating students with disabilities into regular classes. MacMillan School typifies this scenario:

When MacMillan School opened in 1929, visitors from around the world came to see one of the first public schools designed to help children with disabilities. The school, one large brick building, was designed to house disabled students, kindergarten through twelfth grade. After World War II, typical children living within walking distance began attending the school also, but not in the same classes with disabled students. In the 1950s enrollment was over 600. Many students had either cerebral palsy or polio.

Today MacMillan has 262 students in kindergarten through sixth grade. The brick two-story building looks faded and worn by weather, time, and use. Each of its many tall windows has lots of small panes encased in cracked, peeling wood. Inside, the school looks well preserved. Wide walls, fresh white walls, large murals, monthly exhibits of pictures illustrating historical events, and colorful student art give it life.

Ironically, the students with physical disabilities who must use wheelchairs cannot get to the second-floor classrooms. The school has no elevator.

MacMillan has fewer students than other elementary schools in the district. Rumors about closing the school and consolidating to other more modern area schools smolder. Approximately 30 percent of the total 262 students are disabled. They arrive at the school on school buses, some of them after hour-long treks from other parts of the city.

MacMillan offers disabled students a full range of services, including physical therapy, occupational therapy, a small heated pool for therapy, four full-time reading specialists, a math teaching assistant, and some 63 full and part-time aides and volunteers. There are ten regular or "neighborhood" classes, seven special education classes, and two "pre-first or developmental classes for kids with emotional problems who could not handle first grade." The regular classes generally have more than 26 students in each. The special classes have 12 or fewer.

Ironically, the school has never consciously promoted mainstreaming. Some youngsters make it into the mainstream, but only when teachers work out the integration informally between themselves. One great barrier to integration has been the building's inaccessibility. But there are other barriers as well.

At MacMillan we heard school staff talk of "mainstreaming" as "treating everyone the same." But when we observed school life we noticed a number of ways in which disabled students are boxed out of the mainstream.

It is assumed that all students have the necessary skills by which to mingle, tease, joke, and talk with peers. Yet many of these kids have never had the chance to mingle before. One of the teachers was very pessimistic about the degree of social interaction going on in the classroom: "Of course the social stuff is a big consideration but the kids with disabilities don't socialize. They don't mix academically either and really don't mix in anything."

In one sixth-grade class, four "integrated" disabled students have their desks together in a cluster. When the class breaks up into work groups, the disabled students are generally isolated together. When the class goes outside for ten or twenty minutes after lunch, the disabled students either do not go outside at all or they do something by themselves.

When the class had a field trip, the student in a wheelchair had his own bus. Timmy rode on his own special bus. It was large enough for the whole class, but the class rode on a regular bus and Timmy on one with a lift. After the buses pulled to the curb by the courthouse (the destination of this field trip), the driver of the special bus got Timmy down and wheeled up to the rest of the waiting class members.

In other words, teacher deals get disabled students into regular class-rooms, but significant barriers to social integration still remain.

At this same school we met a teacher aide named Al McGregor, who is himself disabled and who is counteracting many of these barriers to integration. He spends much of his spare time in the school counseling disabled students, helping them build up their self-esteem and their confidence so that they can succeed in the mainstream of society. "Most of these kids have never seen somebody my age that's in a wheelchair and independent doing what I do. Because back a number of years ago when I first started, it took me about six months to convince the kids that I was one of their teachers. Because in their heads you can only be a teacher if you are walking around." For several years Al has taken a group of his students on a field trip to his apartment, where he serves them lunch. "I feel better about teaching kids that way. I feel I have more to give by doing that than, in some ways, what I do here. In effect, anybody could sit here and do what I do. But not anybody could take the kids on a field trip like that and show them what it's like and what it's all about. It's really kind of a high for me."

Al also counsels nondisabled students. When he sees a student showing negative attitudes toward somebody because of their disability, he is not afraid to speak up. "If it's on a one-to-one situation and a kid does something, then I have the opportunity. I'll call him over and sit down with him and talk to him a little bit. And nine times out of ten, he won't do that again. I just say, 'Hey, look, I'm different from you, but you have two feet and I've got four wheels.' And that's about it."

When it comes to integrating disabled students into regular classes, Al believes there is a fine line between providing necessary and useful support to students and teachers and being patronizing. He believes that the key principle for teachers to remember is to deal with the disability and any difficulties it may present but not to overemphasize it. There's a risk, Al warns, that the image of a student's disability may so dominate everyone's perception of him or her, that mainstreaming can never succeed. Putting himself in the place of the person who might be mainstreamed, Al remarks, "Deal with me as a person and not with some special thing that's got a problem that you've got to bite your nails over."

The MacMillan case is not unusual. In schools where mainstreaming depends on teacher deals, we often found conflicting forces at work. Where such schools achieved successful integration, it usually depended on one or a few individuals who had practical strategies. Lynn, in her example of Josey cited earlier, knew how to schedule support services in the classroom and how to modify her curriculum. Al McGregor, in the MacMillan School case, knew how to build self-confidence among disabled students and how to help nondisabled students overcome their stereotypes about disabilities.

The obvious problem of the "teacher deals" model is that it runs the risk of leaving students and teachers stranded, unsupported. It heightens the likelihood of failure. At the very least, the lack of systemic support and planning means that integration will have rough spots. As one teacher explains, "It was like 'Let's Make a Deal'—in the first two weeks of school the special-ed teachers would scramble around asking receptive teachers to take some of their kids. Then, two weeks into the term the kids would come into class for the first time and stick out like a sore thumb."

Islands in the Mainstream

If you spend time observing lots of schools, you find out pretty quickly that there is no such thing as a "regular school." More accurately, there are "types" of regular schools. Just as there are types of mainstreaming. Indeed, to understand the different forms mainstreaming takes, you have to understand "types" of schools. One type of mainstreaming is the "self-contained class in a regular school." We observed many such programs. One was actually four classes of students labeled "Severely Emotionally Disturbed" in an inner-city, predominantly black (94%) elementary school. Here, the program we had been told was an instance of "mainstreaming," was at once truly separate from the rest of the school and yet very much reflected the overall culture of this school.

It did so in several ways: student behavior problems were perceived by staff as separate from academic problems. Students with behavior problems were assumed to need behavioral treatment, if you will, "a repair job." That was the purpose of special programming. As one teacher of the four special classes put it, "they are sent to us for behavioral clean-up and if we do our job right . . . we clean up their behavior."

The four special classes were truly separate, both physically and psychologically. All of the teachers, the "regular" and "special" alike, see the special classes and work of "special" teachers as different from the regular. The special class is a place where teachers concentrate much of their time on behavior, thus taking away time that could be spent on academics. Regular class teachers view special class teachers as people who are there to deal with behavior problems. Hence, "you refer kids out for that [for behavior treatment]." Similarly, special class teachers lament the fact that they do not match the regular class's emphasis on academic learning: "There is no way I could run my groups [reading groups] as thoroughly as [the regular class teacher] does." The students perceive the difference between special and regular not so much as a contrast between "behavioral training" and "academic learning" but rather as "less demanding" versus "more demanding." As one special student explains, "They think that when you go to the Learning Center that it will be easy and you won't have to do so much work. It's true. Ms. D.'s class [a regular class] does a bunch of work. It is easier down here." In the special classes, which operate on a token economy behavior modi-fication model, students can earn points that can be exchanged for the opportunity to spend time in a game room, in recreation.

It was clear that neither the principal nor most of the "regular staff" perceive the four special classes as an integral part of the total school environment. The four classes are called the Learning Center. It is as if the Learning Center operates as a minischool or a school within a school. The teachers act as a tightly knit "team," in many ways self-sufficient, and thus isolated.

In this inner-city school, "mainstreaming" had two meanings. Some people said the students in the special classes were mainstreamed in the sense that their schooling occurred in a regular school. For others main-streaming meant integrating the labeled students back into regular classes.

We visited other "self-contained programs" in other schools. In most cases, these were for students labeled as "severely" disabled—for exam-ple, severely retarded or autistic. Like our first example, integration meant essentially that special classes were located in regular schools.

But the schools and the participants in them are different from each other. One example that seems to fit best into the category of "islands in the mainstream" is a class for severely disabled (autistic) youngsters. The following is a slightly edited and much condensed description of the program and its place in the school as drawn from our observer's case study:

As picture puzzles go, it is a large one. Matt works on it intently. He stands at a table in the back of the classroom and shifts his weight, back and forth, from one leg to the other. Occasionally he mumbles something inaudibly. The jigsaw puzzle box lid with the picture of a fall landscape leans against the wall at the back of the table. In front it looks as though the same picture had fallen, shattered into hundreds of cardboard shards. Oranges, yellows, browns, all of the autumnal hues splotched about on odd-shaped pieces of curves and knobs.

Matt stares at the just-begun jigsaw puzzle. He picks up one piece and turns it quickly round and round with his fingers. His actions seem to speak with an eloquent ambivalence which Matt cannot say in words. "It must fit together. The piece belongs somewhere. Or is my persistence misplaced? I've fit so few together so far. But I have fit a few. I found a corner here, and several pieces of sky. More will come."

As I watch his silent struggle, I find myself thinking more about Matt. He is one of six students in the class. All are labeled as severely autistic. How do they fit together? There are over a thousand other students at the high school which Matt and his classmates attend. Where and how do they hook up with Matt? Then there are Matt's teacher, the principal, the rest of the faculty. How do they color Matt's life? Are all of the pieces there? How much of Matt's puzzle has been finished? And where the hell is the picture on the box lid showing what it should look like when done?

One way to answer the puzzle is to say that in this case mainstreaming is a mission. This class of six severely autistic teenagers is new to Hutton High School this year. It is the first time that students with such severe disabilities have ever attended Hutton. It is one of the first such programs nationally.

You can't ask these students how they feel about their new school, or the typical students who sometimes stare in the halls, or the new requirement and risks. You can't ask because they can't say. But you can imagine how it must be puzzling for them, too.

Occasionally, as I watched the students—in the lunch room, at shop class, or just walking down the long corridors at Hutton—I would be reminded that it wasn't inanimate shapes which adults were moving about to see who fit where. These puzzle pieces were fitting themselves in, finding room for their own odd behavioral bumps and curves. We never just "mainstream." We mainstream students, people. They need to be seen and felt as helping to find their own solutions.

Mel and John are the teacher and teacher's assistant, respectively. The class depends on them for much of its tone and structure. Their planning and performance at the high school have been crucial to the program's success. If the class is to be accepted in the school, they have to become part of the school themselves. Mel decided to become the soccer team's coach. He likes to do it, but it's also a strategy for acceptance.

Let's go back to Matt. Almost eighteen, Matt is the oldest member of the class. He is a good-sized (5′ 10″ or so), well-built, handsome fellow. In many ways his overt behavior is the least bizarre or noticeably different of the class. Matt is a hard worker to the point of compulsiveness. He becomes bothered if asked to switch activities for some reason before a task is completed. Matt is also the only student who still lives in an institution, a fact which is no small source of irritation to Mel. Here is where we see why this case of main-streaming is a kind of mission, at least for the teacher, Mel.

"You want to see what an institution can do to a capable person, Matt's a perfect example. He is so reluctant to do things spontaneously. He's learned *not* to do *anything* unless told. Sometimes he'll want to do something so bad, and it will be something perfectly harmless like stopping in the hall for a drink of water. But instead of just doing it he'll just get agitated and look for me or John. Or in class he might start rocking, but never call out for attention. He'll just sit there and get frustrated until one of us notices. It's really a shame. He's such a reliable and capable kid. It's almost like you have to force him to enjoy himself."

If given direction, Matt can go independently anywhere he needs to in the school. Mel, for example, often gives Matt the key to the classroom and lets him go back early from lunch. It's not a short walk. Matt understands almost everything said to him. He also has some good expressive language, but speaks so softly that you can barely hear him. With his skills, ability to observe and imitate, and generally reticent behavior, Matt has been the easiest student for Mel to integrate into several typical classes. So, he is getting out of the self-contained class once in awhile, *off the island.*

The Dual System

Suppose that a small school district has a child with severe cerebral palsy. The child's parents want her to attend the local neighborhood school. But the child needs an aide in the classroom as well as professional speech, occupational, and physical therapy. The school district could hire the special staff at an annual expense of more than $70,000 per year. That is a lot of money for one child. Or, the school district could consider other options.

One way that many states have attempted to solve this problem is to establish "intermediate school" districts to serve a multidistrict area. Individual districts cooperate in governing the intermediate school district and share in its services, including special education, vocational education programs, computer services, diagnostic services, and so forth. In some instances the intermediate school districts established large regional schools for handicapped students only. The approach precluded mainstreaming. But in other cases the intermediate school districts created special programs located in regular school buildings (the intermediate school district rented space from local districts).

We observed mainstreaming programs where students in intermediate-district-sponsored special education programs were mainstreamed into regular schools and in some instances into regular classroom activities. The model was fraught with problems. We observed one system in which "special students" did not know from one year to the next where their program would be located. Since classroom space was rented each year, and since many of the students were from districts other than the ones in which classrooms were currently located, host districts had little commitment to provide continuity in the form of guaranteed space over a period of years. In one program, the parents complained that because their children were bused long distances to school, they didn't get to know neighborhood children. In this and other programs we observed that the teachers were never quite sure to whom they owed allegiance, to administrators of the intermediate district who hired them or to the building principal where they worked. In one case, the special teachers from the intermediate district had a different salary structure and different holidays from local district teachers. The two groups of teachers had separate faculty meetings as well. We concluded that a major barrier to student integration in one such school was the gulf between the intermediate and local teachers. In perhaps the worse example we saw of a program run by an intermediate school district, a regular school principal explained the degree of misunderstanding and broken communication that can occur if the built-in problems of this model are not constantly addressed:

Each year my involvement has been less and less. The Intermediate takes increasingly more responsibility for the administration. I wish there were more sharing. The Intermediate District teachers have different schedules for holidays, vacations, etc. Sometimes our teachers are resentful that they not only get our holidays because the school is closed but others as well. The

Intermediate program closes one week before ours does in June. So they have the luxury of finishing their reports, doing IEP's, and cleaning their rooms while our teachers are still teaching all day.

Almost exclusively the Intermediate supervisor does the decision making for the program. When the program first began, there was more sharing and openness. Now there is more, if not complete, domination by them. They share very little with us. We are really ignored as far as decision making is concerned.

The relations of regular and intermediate school personnel had deteriorated to one of "we" and "they,"

On the most positive side in this case, the intermediate school district was able to mount a deaf education program in regular elementary, junior, and senior high schools. Profoundly deaf students attended regular schools. In many instances, profoundly deaf students were mainstreamed in regular classes. The intermediate school district provided them with "interpretutors" who could translate the regular class teacher's comments and lectures into sign language. Clearly, such services could be developed and shared by local districts as well as by an intermediate district.

As we have noted thus far, no mainstreaming model is without problems. The dynamic nature of schools as social settings and the fact that disabilities are so often defined stereotypically virtually guarantee that in any type of mainstreaming situation problems arise. In each of the subsequent chapters we discuss specific strategies for making mainstreaming work successfully, despite all of the potential problems and pitfalls.

Unconditional Mainstreaming

In most schools, mainstreaming has not wrought basic changes in how schools function. For the most part, teachers still seem remarkably isolated from each other; most "regular teachers" regard students with disabilities as the province of special teachers—one hears phrases like "They have the training, we don't." Some administrators feel that pressures for mainstreaming simply complicate and make more difficult the tasks of operating a school.

But despite this picture, we found a number of exceptions to the rule. We observed school programs where mainstreaming had significantly altered the school's culture. In one school, for example, students with severe and profound disabilities, such as autism and severe retardation, attended small classes with nondisabled students. The school seemed to operate as if successful mainstreaming were its overriding concern. What some schools took for granted, this school pondered carefully. Teachers avoided using labels like "handicapped" and "disabled." Instead, they spoke of children who were just learning to walk or children who as yet had learned only a few signs and were not yet talking. Parents participated in staff hiring committees, in long-term planning groups, and as salespeople to convince area school districts to adopt a similar model of integration. Parent workers took information about the classroom curriculum into parents' homes and enlisted the help of parents in carrying over classroom gains. Students with disabilities were never grouped together for purposes of instruction. Such policies and practices were no accident.

In this school, integration occurs in each classroom. It occurs with administrative support, within a context that places a premium on mainstreaming, and as part of a plan. If staff are extraordinarily careful in how they refer to students, that is, careful with labels, then this reflects the staff's consideration. If parents are involved, this simply demonstrates the fact that the staff and parents value such involvement. Here, mainstreaming is not an afterthought, not merely an add-on program. Rather, here mainstreaming exists because teachers, administrators, and parents decided they wanted it and because they consciously and carefully planned how they could best make it happen.

In settings where the commitment to mainstreaming was unconditional, teachers and staff spoke of integration and learning as correlated goals. We did not hear staff try to disown certain children as another staff's responsibility, nor was mainstreaming perceived as something being tried out on an experimental basis. In the eyes of staff, mainstreaming could not fail. Rather, it was "a given" of the settings, just like gym, recess, grouping of children by their ages, and a five-and-one-half-hour school day were givens.

In many ways what seemed to make mainstreaming possible in these planned settings was not only the prior planning but also the presence of a problem-solving attitude. Note, for example, how the teachers in one integrated classroom discussed strategies for dealing with a student who, apparently in order to get attention, sometimes hit other students in the class:

"What she wants is attention," Mary said. "If we give her a long lengthy explanation for why she shouldn't do what she is doing, we may be giving her just what she wants. And, also, I think we should say a quick no and then walk away before she has a chance to grin."

"She has an incredible grin," Heidi added laughingly. But then Heidi wondered, "Does she need 'No, you can't hit kids,' or is 'No' enough?"

"Let's keep the verbal stuff short," Sally argued.

"Well, but should we say 'No' and then take her in the hall?" Heidi asked.

"Well, we should say 'No' real quickly," Sally said. "We don't need to say she doesn't need to be with kids."

"Well," Heidi said, "we could take her in the hall, and if she knows that she shouldn't be hitting kids, then that is the one activity, hitting of kids, for which we should take her in the hall."

"Is that the only thing you take her into the hall for?" Shana asked. "Because the other day I took her in the hall for writing on the table."

"I think only for hitting," Heidi said. Sally nodded her head.

Then Heidi asked, "What should we say when she is in the hall? Should we say, 'Are you ready to come back now?' "

"You should give it a minute or two," Shana suggested.

"The other day," Heidi recalled, "she came back into our meeting and she hit me, and so I put her back out there, and then I said, 'You can come back when you are ready.' So the second time when she came back in, she was fine."

"She is just as interested in the negative attention as in the positive," Shana argued. "One is as good as the other."

"It's not as though she doesn't know the difference," Heidi said. "Like today all she wanted was negative. She kept putting on her purposeful witchie voice."

"But she looked real happy getting on the bus," Shana noted.

"Ya, she got on that bus and said, 'Boy, I really gave them a run for their money today.' "

"She can be perfectly charming, like today, when I had her sitting down on the milk crate," said Shana. "I went away and she got up and walked over and offered to help you and Jamie. She really knows what she is up to."

At the end of that staff meeting, the teachers agreed on a concerted strategy to address Peggy's tough behaviors. If she behaved negatively, they would simply say "No," with no explanation. They were convinced that she fully understood what was acceptable and unacceptable behavior and the why of it all. They wanted to avoid reinforcing her "difficult behaviors."

The teachers used a number of behavioral terms in reference to working with Peggy. They spoke of "reinforcing" and "negative" behaviors. Yet these words came out unobtrusively and not as part of a jargon-filled conversation. The teachers did not use terms like *extinguished behaviors, behavioral technology, contingency management,* and so forth. Indeed, such language would seem out of place in this environment. It would create a sense of the children's being manipulable objects. In fact, the teachers did adhere to a behavioral approach, namely that actions have antecedents and consequences and that all people respond to different stimuli (i.e., treatment, actions). Yet they practice this belief in the context of a very personal and consciously humanistic environment. The teachers were intent upon creating a warm, supportive environment in which children were responded to individually yet also, if necessary, in a conscious and systematic fashion. The teacher's approach to Peggy exemplified this. Their behaviors were no more random or unpredictable than hers.

In this situation, mainstreaming was not a privilege or something that the teachers were trying on an experimental basis. Rather, mainstreaming was a basic tenet of the classroom. Peggy belonged in the classroom, difficult behavior and all, just as did the other children. During the staff's discussion, there was never even a hint that Peggy might be too difficult or that she could not be successfully mainstreamed. She was in the mainstream and that was simply how the school operated. It was what we might call unconditional mainstreaming.

In some other schools, particularly at the high school level, we observed self-contained classes as well as resource room programs where the presence of disabled students in the school, if not always in regular classes, was similarly regarded as a standard operating procedure. In each of these cases, what distinguished this form of mainstreaming from others was the degree of administrative support, the problem-solving attitude throughout the staff, the frequency of discussions by teachers, administrators, and parents on how to make mainstreaming more effective, and careful documentation within the school of progress with individual students. This latter factor proved important, because it enabled staff to point to the program and say, "See, it works. We even have evidence."

CONCLUSION

As educators we have two choices with respect to mainstreaming. We can sit back and say, "Show us the proof that it works, give us the evidence." In this case we render ourselves mere observers. We can let others bear the responsibility of determining what mainstreaming is and how it occurs. Or, we can participate in defining mainstreaming, in one of the forms described above, in some combination of these forms, or in some alternative form. We can watch others give mainstreaming its social meaning or we can ourselves attribute meaning to it.

The principal arguments in favor of mainstreaming suggest that integration benefits students and, ultimately, the society more than segregation does:

- Integration creates the circumstances under which students with disabilities can be treated as normally as possible, where they are least likely to encounter stigma; students with disabilities may still encounter prejudice, stereotyping, and discrimination in integrated situations as in segregated ones, but integration affords at least the opportunity for these to be countered and even eradicated.
- Integrated settings suggest that we can explore means of providing educational services to disabled and nondisabled students together; in this sense, integration scorns the limits inherent in deciding that some students cannot benefit from being around other students.
- If integration can work successfully for severely disabled students in some communities and in certain schools, then logic requires us to ask why it cannot succeed for all students in all schools.

In this introductory chapter we have attempted to define the issues that revolve around mainstreaming. We have described its complexity, its many meanings, and its principal forms. As even this preliminary view of our observational findings suggests, we see much in mainstreaming about which to be enthusiastic. We have seen a teacher aide challenging students' stereotypes about the abilities and disabilities of a person in a wheelchair. We have seen teachers who spend as much time and creative energy on figuring out how to get one student not to hit another as a group of teachers might spend on planning how to introduce a difficult mathematical problem. We have seen a way of organizing special education services—albeit one with some problems—so that profoundly deaf students can attend regular schools. We have seen autistic students attending regular schools.

The fact that mainstreaming typically takes on four forms suggests that we must concern ourselves with knowing rather precisely what we mean by the terms *mainstreaming* or *integration*, and with deciding which form to promote. To summarize from our earlier discussion, the four types of mainstreaming are:

1. *Teacher deals.* In this model, administrators and the educational system do not provide support for mainstreaming or, at least in any significant way, participate in it. They may recognize it, even speak positively about it, but its life depends upon the individual teachers who make it happen.
2. *Islands in the mainstream.* This type refers to those situations in which special education programs (usually self-contained classes or related services) are located in the regular school building but are perceived and treated as separate from the mainstream of school life.
3. *The dual system.* When intermediate school districts locate programs in regular school buildings they often operate as if they were parallel rather than integrated school programs. They are educationally, psychologically, and administratively separate. Unlike the "islands" model, they have more formidable barriers to overcome in order to achieve real integration.
4. *Unconditional mainstreaming.* In this type, administrators, teachers, and parents combine to create a consciously thought out and supported version of integration.

Throughout this book we use the terms *mainstreaming* and *integration* to refer to a broad range of situations, some positive and some negative, some that would fall into the "unconditional mainstreaming" format and others that appear more like the "teacher deals," "islands," or "dual system" types, and some that have to do with mainstreaming of disabled students in regular classrooms while others concern integrating self-contained programs into the life of regular schools. The range in our evidence is unavoidable, for the discussion throughout is based on real situations that we have observed. Hence, the book is about integration in regular classes but it is equally about integration in regular schools. As we found, for a severely disabled student, integration into the daily life of a regular school may be as challenging and as important as integration of a mildly disabled student in a regular class. Whatever the particular situations we choose to discuss in the pages ahead, our main goal is to elaborate on the fourth type of integration, which we have termed "unconditional mainstreaming."

In each of the succeeding chapters we will ask not whether mainstreaming works but rather how it works. More specifically, we will examine practical strategies that parents, teachers, principals, and district-level administrators are using effectively to make mainstreaming work. Some of the strategies seem rooted in common sense. Others seem ingenious. They all confirm the potential of mainstreaming.

2

The Principal's Role
in Mainstreaming

ROBERT BOGDAN AND DOUGLAS BIKLEN

Our observations substantiate what other researchers have found—
the principal is crucial to the success of any school program. Principals
make a difference in mainstreaming (Davis, 1977; Gage, 1979; and Robson, 1981). Some programs may succeed without the active support and
involvement of building principals. But a program cannot succeed where
the principal is opposed, or negatively disposed, to mainstreaming.

Why would a principal be for mainstreaming? Some principals are
motivated by moral and legal reasons—mainstreaming is right. Some we
met had close relationships with people who had disabilities (e.g., they
themselves, or a relative or friend had a disability) and felt personally
committed to maximizing the opportunities for those with disabilities.
One principal told us she was dedicated to heterogeneity among her
students as a method of teaching about life. To her, mainstreaming was
synonymous with good education. But principals, more than any other
respondents to our questions, gave practical reasons for mainstreaming.

In talking to principals, we were amazed to find that the same objective conditions could be used on the one hand as a practical reason not
to mainstream and on the other hand as a practical reason *for* doing it.
Let's look at two such contrasting situations:

Case A: Ms. Able is the principal of a six-hundred-student middle school
that faces declining enrollment. The decreasing number of students plus the
budget cuts has led to rumors that the school is expected to close. Because of

incidents in the neighborhood after school, Ms. Able is concerned that the school is getting a reputation of being "out of hand." There is some indication that middle-class parents are increasingly sending their children to local private schools. She defines her job as stabilizing the school and attracting a higher percentage of the middle-class students. Ms. Able believes children with disabilities will contribute to the school's reputation as a place for problems. She has made it clear that she does not want more labeled children in her school.

In addition to this image issue, Ms. Able says she has "enough to handle" (decreasing enrollments and decreasing budgets). She doesn't need additional worries such as administering the special arrangements necessary for children with disabilities.

Case B: Mr. Brim is the principal of Mesa High School located in the same district as Ms. Able's middle school. In fact, Ms. Able's school is a feeder school for the Mesa High School. There are three other high schools in the district and there is intense competition between the schools. This competition is not only in sports but in getting scarce resources. Each principal vies for personnel and money. Mr. Brim has some of the same problems that Ms. Able is facing. There has been a declining enrollment and his budget has been cut. In addition, Mesa High School has a problem in regard to racial balance. Forty percent of its students are minorities, a situation that could result in court-ordered desegregation. Mr. Brim has taken as a challenge improving the quality of his school and thereby attracting the better students who might otherwise go elsewhere.

Mr. Brim embraced the idea of mainstreaming. In fact, he has pursued the development of special programs in his school. The school has the first high school learning disability program in the city as well as programs for students with autism and students who are moderately, developmentally delayed.

Mr. Brim sees mainstreaming as a way of helping him solve his problems rather than a way of compounding them. By encouraging the development of programs, he sees himself bringing more resources and more students to the school. Rather than seeing it as tarnishing the school's image he sees the program as enhancing it. Because some of the children with disabilities are outside of the geographic area served by Mesa High School, he sees the programs as public relations for the brothers and sisters of children with disabilities and their neighbors, hoping that they will think of transferring to the school as part of a voluntary busing plan. Mr. Brim is also developing high school vocational programs that will take advantage of the mainstreaming programs as part of the training of high school students in health services.

The intention of telling the stories of Able and Brim is not to diminish the real problems faced by Ms. Able. The situations are much more complicated than we present them. But, factual circumstances aside, there is a distinct difference in the perspectives of Ms. Able and Mr. Brim. Mr. Brim attempts to use the district's mainstreaming thrust to solve existing problems. Ms. Able sees mainstreaming as compounding her problems. Principals are for mainstreaming when they can see it benefiting the school as a whole and if they can work out ways of using it to accomplish their own goals.

The promainstreaming principal is optimistic, the person with the half-filled glass, the person with the better mouse trap, the person who can envision opportunity from different perspectives.

SELF-EDUCATION

Who's in Charge?

Whom do special education and students with disabilities belong to? For years principals were taught that special education belonged to someone else, the specialist—it was usually located somewhere else too, in a segregated special school. Further, with the establishment of directors of special education in central offices across the country, even if programs for the disabled were in regular schools, principals have been encouraged to leave the responsibility for special education to the experts.

We found, however, that successful mainstreaming entails the principal's taking charge. Students with disabilities have to be considered as belonging to the school first. The specialist down at the central office comes second. Just as principals bear responsibility for nondisabled students and their programming in their buildings, so too must they assume that kind of responsibility toward the mainstreamed student. The principal, by embracing special education, conveys to the rest of the school that "this student belongs here." In some schools we visited, this take-charge attitude of the principal in regard to his or her responsibility for disabled children was present. In others, it was not. Symbolic of the latter, one observer asked a principal how many students he had in his school. The principal responded, all too characteristically, "Four hundred thirty-three and then fifty-two handicapped." This "them and us" attitude at the principal level undermines the basic focus of mainstreaming.

Principals who demonstrate a commitment to mainstreaming tend to take the lead in selling the concept to the various school constituencies, including students, teachers, support staff, parents, district officials, and the public. Their effectiveness in building support for integration is directly proportional to their ability to work with each group. For example, administrators who regard parents as intruders or as a necessary annoyance will likely have more complaints from parents. Parents will feel alienated. Parents' ideas about how to make integration work will be lost. Parents as allies and salespeople of the program will be lost. In the chapter on parents we examine effective strategies by which principals and parents can collaborate in integration. What we found and now suggest is that principals need both a positive orientation and the practical strategies to implement it.

On Being a Good Example

Mr. Peters is a thirty-five-year-old, lively, highly motivated junior high school principal who supports mainstreaming in his school. In fact, last year he volunteered his school to the central office, which was looking for a place to put two "trainable mentally retarded" classes that were previously located in a segregated self-contained facility. He has been conscious of these students' isolation, and this year he has been working with the teachers to integrate the students more fully. He has facilitated the students' integration into gym, the lunchroom, and industrial arts. He has further plans for integration for the future.

While in many ways Mr. Peters is an advocate for mainstreaming, he is unaware that his own way of talking to and behaving toward those labeled "trainable" gives messages that inhibit mainstreaming. Observe, for example, his encounter in the hall during class change with Billy, a thirteen-year-old student in one of the classes mentioned earlier:

Billy is walking up one side of the hall, going to an integrated shop class. He is accompanied by a teacher's aide, Ms. Andersen. Mr. Peters is walking down the other side of the hall when he sees Billy.

Billy does not have a hearing impairment, but Mr. P. talks to him as if he does. In a very loud voice he says, "How was the trip to the vocational program?" Mr. Peters has a big smile on his face and appears to be self-conscious in Billy's presence. Many people are looking at Mr. Peters and Billy because it is unusual for the principal to stop someone in the middle of the busy hall to talk.

Billy is red in the face and grinning ear to ear. Mr. Peters continues, "You go down town." He is still speaking loudly. He puts his hand on Billy's shoulder and gives a patting motion. He pronounces his words as if he were talking to a non-English speaker. He talks in broken English. Billy, who now has his head down and is blushing, responds, "Yha."

Mr. Peters remarks further, "Going down to shop hey. Hey, I saw the bird feeder you are making and it is absolutely fantastic. You're going to have to go into business." Turning to the teacher's aide, Mr. P. continues, "Did you see Billy's bird house? Fantastic. If it were big enough, it would be nice enough to live in yourself."

Then Mr. Peters lowers his voice, speaking to Ms. Andersen as if Billy weren't present, "Did you talk to Billy's parents? They wanted to see you about his bus schedule."

Ms. Andersen responds, "Yes, I did."

Then Mr. Peters, again in a loud voice, concludes the conversation, "Okay, good—take care. 'Bye Billy."

No matter how well-meaning, most people feel ill at ease and self-conscious in the presence of those with disabilities. The disability takes on exaggerated proportions. It can stand in the way of treating naturally the person behind the disability. Fortunately, through contact with particular people with disabilities the self-conscious, ill-at-ease behavior passes. With enough contact, people can overcome this tendency completely.

Mr. Peters has not. In the encounter we just observed, he exhibits many of the behaviors of a person uncomfortable with disabilities. These behaviors include

- Praising excessively—people who feel ill at ease often exaggerate their praise of what the person with the disability does.
- Treating as a child—praising excessively is just one of a series of actions that fits the pattern of treating a disabled person as a child. Speaking in a condescending, all-knowing way does this as well.
- Speaking loudly—a person who has one disability (e.g., mental retardation) does not usually have others (e.g., hearing impairment).
- Being overly familiar—use of familiar names, touching and putting hands on a person with whom you are not particularly familiar.
- Talking about the person to another in front of the person as if the person is an object.
- Joking, as a way of avoiding a person.
- Singling the person out by disability unnecessarily.

When Mr. Peters did these things he thought nothing of them. In fact, he thought he was being friendly, showing his interest. Often students do not interpret these gestures negatively. Students may not feel self-conscious, embarrassed, and ridiculed. In some cases the student may enjoy such interaction. But as the leader of the school, the principal provides an important role model. Such treatment tells the rest of the school that the student with a disability should not be treated seriously. It also encourages the student with a disability to assume the role of the clown or of the child. People tend to live up to others' expectations. Thus, treating a person stereotypically may result in producing stereotyped behaviors. Be aware of the subtle ways in which gestures and conversation tell others how to think.

There are some other ways in which principals can present a good example. For example, it is typical for people to see a disability as the cause of bad things that happen. All students, classes, and teachers have problems, but many times when students with disabilities have problems these are erroneously linked to the disability rather than just being thought of as problems. In some areas students with disabilities have fewer problems—students in wheelchairs cannot run in the halls, or climb on roofs. But they can have wheelchair races.

Don't Leave It to the Experts

Maribeth Allen was born with severe athetoid cerebral palsy. She has normal intelligence, yet she cannot speak. She can make certain sounds. She smiles to say yes and raises her hand. She keeps her mouth closed and looks off to the right to say no. She can communicate other simple messages, such as that she wants to eat, by using American sign language symbols with her hands, but even this is difficult because her movements are rigid and erratic as a result of her severe cerebral palsy. She understands everything said to her. She attends regular classes and has the assistance of a full-time aide in the classroom.

Her teacher has been pushing the evaluation team to approve his recommendation that Maribeth have a computer and voice box to use as an augmentative communication system. The teacher wants this put in the individual education plan. The teacher has discussed this with the parents. They are as enthusiastic about the proposal as the teacher.

This recommendation raises several important issues. Who should decide whether a school district will provide an expensive piece of equipment such as an electronic augmentative communication system to a student as part of the individual education plan (IEP)? The teacher? The principal? The special education director? The assessment and classification team? Should the district have a policy with respect to augmentative communication? How much does the principal need to know about disabled students and augmentative communication in order to get involved in these issues?

Most school districts have policies regarding program equipment. And most districts rely on the judgment of the assessment and classification team to decide when a student needs such equipment as part of the program. It should be noted that special education directors and/or assistant principals may sit on the assessment and classification team. Principals become involved at every stage. If there is resistance in the special education department to the teacher's recommendation, the principal may have to advocate the teacher's proposal. If principals fail to get involved, then they leave such programming decisions exclusively to special educators, even though the actual decision usually hinges on fiscal rather than programmatic considerations. A principal may also have to work with parents during the decision-making period. If the principal is uninformed about such matters, the parents will tend to feel that the principal is not truly committed to students with disabilities.

Obviously, principals cannot know the technical substance of the entire special education field. Yet, events such as the teacher's recommendation of augmentative communication for Maribeth Allen can serve as opportunities to learn. School administrators can learn the basic principles behind augmentative communication in a matter of a half day or day if they know how to ask questions of their staff, if they can get concise information from the special education office, and if they want to be informed. Armed with basic information, including a working understanding of the special language (jargon) of special education, principals can effectively support teachers and enter into decision making, in the same way that they become involved with program development in so-called regular education.

ACCOMMODATIONS

It is ironic that as school administrators have attempted to make schools more accepting of people with disabilities, they have overlooked some of the most visible aspects of the school. We refer to what some people have called the hidden curriculum: unstated aspects of the school that teach us values. Through the hidden curriculum we learn social attitudes about disabilities. This curriculum is "hidden" not because it is not before our eyes, but because it is so much a part of the world of the school that it goes unnoticed, even to those who are most diligent in seeking humanistic and accepting environments for children.

In the next few pages we want to look at some of these pervasive but beyond-our-awareness lessons as they appear in schools. The principal, as head of the school, has a special role in sensitizing others to the hidden curriculum. The principal can create a school environment with a different kind of hidden curriculum, one that teaches promainstreaming lessons.

Physical Locations of Classrooms

It is a standard joke among special education personnel that when you go into a school looking for special education programs, try the basement—next to the boiler room. Be it in a basement, in a special wing, in a separate building, or at the end of a dead-end corridor, programs for handicapped students have a tradition of being physically isolated. When integrating students with disabilities, whether they are in a resource room, a self-contained classroom, or regular classes, the exemplary programs are as physically integrated into the school as possible.

Physically integrating students, getting them into the heart of the building, has positive consequences:

- Physical closeness makes mixing with nondisabled students easier. Nondisabled students can drop into class. Students with disabilities have easier access to events and places the typical students go.
- Physical integration provides a tangible message to all in the school that disabled students belong there, they are central to the school, not on the periphery. Thus, this physical integration has symbolic meaning.
- Physical proximity, if arranged properly, encourages all in the school to take disabilities for granted. Being seen regularly, children with disabilities are more likely to be viewed as belonging.
- Physical proximity can also work to break down stereotypes. The hidden message of physical isolation is "these people are different

from us." The message of integration is that they are more like us than different.

Factors other than physical isolation have to be considered in assessing whether the location of a program is conducive to mainstreaming. The general rule is that the class or program should be indistinguishable from other classes in regard to location. Watch locations next to the administrative offices or in special service areas. In one school we visited, the principal was proud of his efforts to integrate a classroom of students who had been brought in as a group from a special school for those labeled "trainable mentally retarded." He wanted to make sure the class was functioning well and was central to the school, so he moved it next door to his office. The message received by the teachers in charge as well as many of the students was that the students in this class were trouble and they needed careful watching. Further, some took the location to mean that the principal was not sure whether these new students really belonged in the school. They thought perhaps he wanted to monitor them carefully so as to make a decision as to whether they would stay.

Another location to avoid is the special service area. Keep programs out of janitorial, cafeteria, or guidance-counseling areas. Again, these are not usual classroom locations. To place special programs in them risks sending an unintended and unfortunate message about students with disabilities.

In schools with programs or classes where integration is taking place, there is a tendency to place such classes together. The reasoning is that teachers can share ideas, help each other out, and in other ways improve programming. While there may be some truth behind this reasoning, placing programs together magnifies the visibility of disabled children and in that way sets them apart. In addition, it promotes the idea that students with disabilities should "be with their own kind."

Architectural Barriers

If a sign was posted on a school entrance "NO BLACKS ALLOWED," anger and protest would result. Such blatant discrimination is no longer tolerated—or is it? Long staircases with no ramps, multiple-story buildings without adequate elevators, bathroom stalls not wide enough for wheelchairs, out-of-reach water fountains and phones, and room markings that cannot be read by touch, tell students with disabilities, teachers with disabilities, and administrators with disabilities, "this building is not for you."

Facilities in which people with disabilities (those in wheelchairs and those who can't see well) do not enjoy full access can cause tremendous humiliation. Architectural inaccessibility forces people with disabilities to rely on others to carry them upstairs or into the bathroom, thus undermining their own sense of dignity and contributing to the idea that they are a burden. Wheelchairs can make a person stand out enough, even without his becoming the center of attraction wherever there is no ramp by which to maneuver.

Many of the schools we visited, although technically accessible, created physical obstacles for people with disabilities. In renovating buildings to modify them for access, architects seldom consult people who use them—people in wheelchairs, for example. Thus, many have flaws that make for impracticality or awkward use. Also, seldom is a building made completely accessible. Certain areas of buildings remain out of reach. In one school we visited, the only way to the auditorium was by stairs. Although it may not seem noteworthy that students in wheelchairs have to be carried upstairs to use the auditorium, this can be devastating to a person trying to assert independence.

While there are many helpful resources available on making a school physically accessible (e.g., Adaptive Environments, Inc., and The National Center for a Barrier Free Environment), an important first step for a principal is to try and see the school environment from the viewpoint of those with disabilities who have to use it. Understanding the importance of this issue as well as the details can motivate the principal into becoming the accessibility watchdog of the environment. While everything cannot be changed at once, the principal can press for physical modifications and can accomplish these changes as part of the integration plan.

Quality of Classrooms

There are also jokes in special education circles about the quality of special education rooms and equipment. One teacher told us, "You can tell the special education rooms by the garage sale furniture. I can't ever remember having a room where the furniture matched or where I didn't have to beg, borrow, or steal to get the basics." While funding for special education has improved—and in many schools this teacher's characterization does not hold—it is important that classes with special education programs do not stand out either in the poor quality of their furnishings or in their superior quality.

With the increased number of students with severe disabilities in the school, and with increases in equipment funds, special education programs are apt to have special equipment. Typewriters with large print, teaching machines, mats, roll boards, wheelchairs, and exercise balls are a few examples. Of course, these objects will be purchased for the disabled students' use but they can easily become a tangible evidence of who is and who is not disabled. Whenever possible, such equipment should not be exclusively designated for the use of students with disabilities. Other students should be encouraged to touch the equipment and, where appropriate, to use it. It is through such contact that the fear and mystery surrounding special equipment lose their powers. Through joint use of the equipment, students with disabilities and typical students can share activities. Students with disabilities can teach those without disabilities the use of the equipment.

STAFF DEVELOPMENT

Teacher Support

A teacher of severely autistic children in a regular elementary school had a problem. The other teachers in the school as well as the administrative staff did not know what she was doing with and for her students. They seemed to steer a wide berth around her. She felt that the other teachers probably regarded her students as a bit strange. After all, each time she took the class to the lunchroom, one of her students would let out a yelp or two. Several others would flap their arms. And still others seemed unable to respond to people who spoke to them. Indeed, they might seem a bit strange. But this teacher desperately wanted the other teachers and staff to understand the children and the education she was providing them.

To accomplish this she needed support. A resource staff person gave her that support. The same support could easily have come from the teacher's principal. The resource staff, part of a roving, regional team, came into the class several times and made videotapes of the students. He recorded classroom activities on videotape. He prepared "before and after" video clips of students. One student who did not know how to hold a piece of chalk, learned to hold it and to write letters. A child who, when she entered the classroom, had been afraid to touch anyone, was shown touching other children and the teacher. A student who had not yet learned to speak intelligible language was shown using sign language.

The teacher then asked for time at a regular faculty meeting to show the videotape and to describe what she was trying to accomplish in the class. Immediately upon showing the videotapes to her fellow teachers and to the administrators, they began to take an interest in her work. They began to ask serious questions about the educational needs of individual students in her class. They even began to suggest having their classes do more common activities with her students. Special education was no longer an odd appendage at this school, it was part of the school.

Integrating Special Education Teachers

Students with disabilities are not the only people who have been segregated, stigmatized, and made to feel that they do not belong. Special education teachers and disability specialists have, by choice, by circumstance, or by habit, been left out of the mainstream of American education. The housing of special education programs in separate buildings or in basements or in special sections of schools meant that teachers who worked with special education students were cast as being different, as not part of the normal teachers' world. Some reacted by building an identity about serving the special, feeling quite comfortable with their angel-of-mercy image and isolated status. Others felt separated but could do nothing about it. After awhile, they gave in to their special status and did not object to regular teachers and administrators when they were told: "You must have so much patience." "You are so giving. I couldn't handle it."

With movement to integrate, the mainstreaming of teachers is as important as mainstreaming for students. This is not a simple matter. Some special education teachers feel comfortable in the role they have been forced to assume. Reinforced by years of being told that they are special and that their students need them, they are sometimes the leaders of the opposition for integration, both opposing the integration for themselves and for their students. In addition, many administrators are so used to thinking of special education teachers as a different species, they often do not know how to bring them into the fold, or for that matter what their place in the school should be.

Compare and contrast these two situations:

Case A: Mary Jones teaches in a deaf education program that is located
in a local public school. She is one of four special education teachers who
make up the program that is administrated by a special intermediate school
district. She is paid by the special district and follows the special district calendar, which means that she has days off when the other teachers in the
building do not, and is supposed to be on duty when the other teachers are
not. The four classes that make up this program are located in one wing of
the school building at the end of the hall. Although many of the deaf children
are integrated, ostensibly in regular school classes, Mary and other teachers of
the deaf, for the most part, stay in their area of the school. At lunch, the
teachers of the deaf always eat together. A few have relationships that go
back to when they worked at a segregated residential program for the deaf.
Lunch conversation sometimes goes back to those good old days. Often, you
can hear the teachers lamenting how it is impossible for regular class teachers
to understand deaf children. Mary and the other teachers are not invited to the
regular teachers' meetings that are held in the school of which their classes
are a part. They do not even have mailboxes in the central office. Mary's
students are more integrated into the mainstream of school life than she is.
Her segregation inhibits their integration.

Case B: Marj Levey is a resource teacher. She is certified in special education. But she and the other special education teachers in the school in which
she works do not have an exclusive relationship. Although her closest friend
in the school is another resource teacher, she is in another wing of the building and both of them have a range of relationships with a variety of school
personnel as well as students and both feel that they are treated just like the
other teachers. If Marj has some free time, she goes to the teachers' room and
chats, sometimes about business (e.g., one of the students she is working
with is having a problem), but most of the time it is a time for just being
social. Marj is invited to, and regularly attends, schoolteachers' meetings.
The school principal knows her well and feels free to involve her in the various school activities. She is not reluctant to get involved, whether for chaper-
oning a dance or serving on a curriculum committee. She coaches the
school's golf team and has daily contact with typical students through this
activity as well as through her other undertakings. When the school play came
up, she volunteered to be one of the main ticket sellers, an activity in which
she got some of her special education students involved. She asks for no special privileges because of the students whom she teaches nor does she expect
to be treated as someone who is different. Her thorough integration into the

school helps the special education students in her classroom make contacts and be more taken for granted.

These vignettes illustrate some conditions and situations that should be fostered in attempts at promoting the integration of special education teachers.

1. Special education teachers should be on the same schedule and calendar as regular teachers.
2. The administration of special education programs should be an integral part of the total school structure and not serve to isolate special teachers from regular teachers.
3. Special education teachers should be invited to, and be expected to attend, regular faculty meetings and social events. Issues that special education teachers are dealing with should be brought up before the faculty as a whole. Isolated special education meetings should be kept to a minimum.
4. Special education teachers should be encouraged by both their physical location and by any other means to be a regular part of the ongoing social and professional life of the teachers in the school. Regular teachers and special education teachers should be given every opportunity and encouragement to mix.
5. Stereotypes, such as the angel-of-mercy image and others that cast the special education teacher as someone who is categorically different from the regular teacher, should be discouraged. Cliches and joking patterns that leave these stereotypes unexamined should be discouraged.
6. Special education teachers should be put on all the mailing lists and receive all school notices, and so on, that regular teachers receive. Similarly, the regular class teachers should get memos, and so forth, that concern special education teachers most directly.
7. Special education teachers should have responsibilities with typical students. They should not be thought of as exclusively serving disabled students.
8. Special efforts should be made to make special education teachers feel at home and a part of school life. Special education teachers should be, for example, given a mailbox that is not different from any other teacher's mailbox. Referring to special education teachers

by their disability assignment ("she's the L.D. teacher") should be discouraged.

9. Special education teachers should be given leadership responsibility in the school (e.g., they should coach teams when appropriate).

10. Regular class teachers should be made aware of the potential isolation and discomfort that special education teachers may feel. Regular class teachers should be encouraged to go out of their way to include them.

11. Exclusive relationships among special education teachers should be discouraged in every way possible.

Staff with Disabilities

Having teachers, administrators, and other staff with disabilities on a faculty can be an important statement to students and adults about mainstreaming. Mainstreaming is usually defined as placing disabled students with their typical peers. In the course of our case studies we met individuals with disabilities working in schools. Although this number was small, they taught us to enlarge our definition of mainstreaming to include enabling disabled adults to participate as staff in schools.

Disabled adults can play a significant part in making mainstreaming happen. The disabled teacher's experiences of growing up disabled can make him or her an effective and credible counselor as well as a resource to students and staff. The importance of the disabled staff member as a role model should not be underestimated. How can students with disabilities work toward a future if they do not have people in their immediate environment to whom they can look as illustrative of what is possible?

Typical students and teachers learn lessons, too, that people with disabilities function well in society, that they can fill positions of responsibility, that the nondisabled person need not be fearful, that you can overcome any discomfort you might have in being around disabled people, and that people with disabilities have an important place in schools.

Too often, affirmative action programs are approached with the spirit of doing the minority a favor. In talking to staff with disabilities, we learned of the benefits that accrue to students and schools when disabled adults are part of the mainstreaming plan. Their limitations offer advantages.

DESIGNING AND RECORDING CHANGE

Keeping Data

How do you know change when you see it? We like to think that we can recognize change when it occurs. But can we? The most basic principle of research is to record current, or what we often call baseline, data—this stage of research is also frequently called the pretest—and then to contrast that with posttest or experimental data. That is, we gather information about our subjects before we treat them to a new educational strategy or approach and then we gather information about their performance after the fact. We then infer, as best we can, the effects of the intervention. When schools gather reading, math, and other aptitude data from year to year, they track student performance. By comparing a student's performance of one year with that of another, we can examine the changes that have occurred.

We do not always keep similar before-and-after data about programmatic or organizational changes. So it is with integrating disabled students into regular public schools. How can we know change when we see it if we do not gather data? What kind of data should we collect? If principals are really going to make a difference in promoting integration, they need to collect data, concerning the following, for example:

- The student who has literally no skills for independent living who has learned to use the local bus system, to cross streets safely, to shop at the grocery store, and to ask for help when needed.
- The student who used to pull other students' hair but has learned to not do that.
- The student who had seemed so alone but has developed some skills at making friends.
- The student who does not talk but who is reading.
- The student who has never been educated alongside nondisabled students but is participating in a modified vocational education program.
- The speech therapy staff who have worked with teachers to integrate speech therapy into the academic curriculum where appropriate.
- The special education teacher who has become the soccer or golf team coach (an example of staff integration).

• The parent-teacher association that now includes parents of disabled
and nondisabled students, special and regular teachers working side
by side.

Listening to Students

Several years ago we helped to make a film about mainstreaming.
While preparing a particular scene in a high school, we heard a memorable
conversation between a physically disabled student and a nondisabled
student. We wished that we had captured it on film.

Peter, the nondisabled student, remarked to us, "I think I have good
attitudes. I always like to help John." The John he referred to was the
physically disabled student who was within earshot.

Peter's statement irritated John. "That really makes me mad," John
remonstrated. "You always think of me as someone who needs help. You
never stopped to think that I might be able to give help. You never ask
me for help. You think that just because I can't walk, I'm the one that
needs the help."

Such encounters are not altogether unusual. And they certainly are
not comfortable. But they do educate. What better way to learn positive
attitudes about disabilities, or what stereotypes we harbor and should
dispense with, than to learn firsthand.

In this case, the school principal heard the entire encounter. For him,
and for principals in general, such incidents provide excellent material
for staff and student development. Of course principals can develop a
practical awareness of the attitudinal issues simply by meeting with disabled and nondisabled students and hearing what they have to say. What
are nondisabled students thinking about disabilities? What kinds of stereotyping most bother students with disabilities? Principals can lead the
way in exploring these matters.

ATTITUDES

Stereotyped Images of the Disabled

One evening, one of us was watching Walt Disney's *Treasure Island*
on television with his eight-year-old son, Jono, and his friend Jeremy,
who was spending the night. At one point in the film, Jeremy asked Jono

whether a particular character was a good guy or a bad guy. Jono replied, "If they look bad, they are bad."

This connection between physical appearance and danger is lost to most people concerned with issues of disability. A careful review of *Treasure Island* and thousands of other films, comic strips, and books reveals a connection between physical and mental disability and danger. Throughout our culture, people with missing limbs, scars, patched eyes, palsied faces, and irregular movements are cast as menacing monsters who murder, maim, and in other ways run roughshod over others. Children learn to fear those with disabilities early in their lives. Of course, this imagery has also made its way into schools. At Halloween parties, children come dressed as hunchbacks, as menacing, hook-armed pirates, and as plotting, wart-nosed, lame witches. School libraries are filled with books that cast people with disabilities in stereotypical ways.

Portrayals as dangerous, sinister, or evil are not the only stereotypical depictions of people with disabilities in literature and the mass media. Disabled persons are often characterized as pitiable and pathetic, objects of violence, "atmosphere" (i.e., an interesting, provocative object or curiosity), "super crip," someone to laugh at, a burden, nonsexual, or incapable of fully participating in everyday life.

What can be done about this imagery? We do not recommend censorship. We do not believe that *Grimm's Fairy Tales, Treasure Island, Of Mice and Men,* and *Peter Pan* and the many Disney films with handicappist imagery should be banned (Biklen & Bailey, 1979). The impact of such hidden messages can be minimized, we believe, through discussion and education. Just as some students learn to be analytical and skeptical about TV commercials, so can they learn to see through stereotypical messages about people with disabilities.

Naming Programs

Whenever possible, programs for students with special needs should *not* have titles that point out the participant's diagnostic category. Titles such as "learning-disabled program" or "trainable mentally retarded" promote labeling, stereotyping, and avoidance by others. One difficult task that students with special needs have is developing ways of thinking about themselves which preserve self-esteem. Program labels often make students feel bad about themselves. We interview a number of students who uniformly were ashamed of being associated with such titles as "special education" and even "resource room." The history of special education is a history of euphemisms. It seems that every time a clinical designation develops a bad name, the name is changed. Thus, when "idiots," "morons," and "feeble-minded" became objectionable, the phrases "severe, moderate, and mild mental retardation" and "developmental disabilities" were coined. Institutions for people so labeled have experienced corresponding name changes. In spite of these changes, the negative connotation of the old words soon caught up with the new.

The students we talked with appreciated not having special names attached to their programs. They preferred to be known as being in "Mrs. Thompson's Program," for example, than being in the "Resource Room Program." They did not like to be associated with the title "Special Education" in any form. One school had a room with the words "Special Projects" on the door. While the meaning of the designation was unclear even to the observers, it was clear to the students; clear and negative. They didn't want to be associated with it.

If there is some uniform system of designating classrooms in a school, classes with special education students in them should have the same designations. A resource room should not be referred to as "a resource room" but rather as "room 202." One student asked us, "Why did they have to call Mrs. Thompson's program a resource room? Why not just call it a study hall?" Such nonstigmatizing names should replace more clinical designations.

Students are so sensitive to the special-name issue that they often evaluate teachers on the degree to which the teachers single them out by using special education designations. One child told an observer how much she disliked the gym teacher because she would give directions such as, "All special education students please move into the locker rooms." Another student told us how she and her friends grimaced each time someone on the school's loudspeaker identified special education classes, even if by a euphemism.

The principal can serve a key role in eliminating such embarrassing incidents. In the case of the loudspeaker, this can be done by direct monitoring. In other cases it can be done by reminder or example. There is a tendency to let such references slide, thinking that they really do not matter. Our observations suggest that they do matter greatly to students. Teachers and other school personnel are sensitive to being brought to task for these seemingly unimportant references. Tact is important in remedying the situation. Orders usually create anger. Explanation, education that appeals to students' feelings, often works best.

Name-Calling

Imagine a school that serves disabled and nondisabled students. And imagine that in this school one is not referred to as *autistic, mentally retarded, emotionally disturbed, physically disabled, learning disabled,* or in any other way disabled. Rather, the staff refer to students by their names and, when necessary, refer to their learning needs or learning difficulties (e.g., John has difficulties in expressive language; Mary has difficulty with fine motor coordination).

The point is simple. When adults use labels, students pick them up. If adults use language that humanizes and individualizes rather than categorizes students, students will themselves be less likely to use the labels. We have observed that principals can provide "language leadership" by setting an example and by openly discussing the labeling issue with staff.

In the course of one of our integration studies, we spoke with a four-year-old girl who attends a school which integrates severely autistic and nondisabled students. This girl has no disability. While talking with her, one of us used the term *handicapped*. She asked, "What does handicapped mean?" We explained the term in a way that we thought she might understand. "Well, it means that a person has a hard time walking, or needs to use a wheelchair, or has a hard time talking, or has a hard time understanding things, or a hard time hearing or seeing," we said, "Oh, you mean like John. He can't walk," she told us. "We have two kids in our class who have handicaps."

Her response surprised us. First, because she has three students in her class who have severe disabilities. And second, it occurred to us that she had attended this unique school program for nearly six months and had not heard the term *handicapped* used before. Our own observers at the school also did not hear the term used during their six months of observations. Besides her academic program, this student was learning that some of her fellow students had various differences, like not being able to walk or talk, yet she had learned to see these as qualities of the students and not as all-defining. She did not see these other students as "the handicapped." We asked her about these students and she was able to tell us about them as people, what they like and do not like, where they live, and what they are learning, and so on.

CONCLUSION

We began this chapter with accounts of two principals, one who viewed mainstreaming/integration as another potential headache and another who sees only opportunities. Ironically, both showed a variety of other problems in their schools (e.g., declining enrollments, integration/desegregation concerns, school image problems). Yet they drew different conclusions about whether or not to support the integration of students with disabilities into their schools.

The point is obvious. Principals have a choice, to support or not support such integration efforts. And clearly, principals who choose to support integration programs can do so in practical ways. Our research of integration efforts suggests some major areas in which principals can support integration:

• Self-Education. Principals, like anyone else, can effect change only if they are willing to change. In other words, principals must have a plan for organizational change, but they must also regard the whole process as a learning experience. If they are not open to change, they cannot expect to find such openness among the rest of the school staff or in the community around them. Principals can pursue the goal of personal change by (a) learning about special education as opportunities arise, (b) by learning from disabled students and other people with disabilities, and (c) by asking others (e.g., parents, other administrators, and teachers) to review their integration efforts.

• Accommodations. Some people have feared that mainstreaming might be used as an excuse for saving money, for making no special efforts on behalf of students with disabilities. Certain measures that principals can take will cost money. Yet these measures cannot be avoided. Often they can be accomplished in a cost-effective fashion if carefully planned. These measures include such things as making a building architecturally accessible and providing for a quality classroom setting (i.e., providing large-type books for visually impaired students and amplification equipment for students with hearing impairments). Program location also plays a central role in facilitating or inhibiting integration. If special programs are located in school basements, in segregated wings of school buildings, or in otherwise lesser or different settings, we communicate the message that the teachers and students in these settings are also different, set apart. Principals can facilitate integration by (a) locating special programs in the physical mainstream, (b) scheduling educational services for students with disabilities in a fashion that is consistent with the scheduling patterns for all students in the school, and (c) by referring to special programs in terms similar to those used for regular education (e.g., room 101, art, music, vocational education, as compared to "the severe and profound room," 'trainable art," "special music," or "educable voc. ed.").

- Staff Development. New programs require staff support. Principals can elicit staff interest and involvement by taking the initiative in (a) hiring staff who have disabilities, (b) providing staff education related to integration, (c) providing consulting teacher and other support to teachers who participate in the integration efforts, and (d) through systematic strategies to integrate "special" and "regular" education staff of the school.
- Designing and Recording Change. Principals who have a plan to support integration and who gather data, even personal, highly anecdotal data, throughout the process of implementing integration are better able to build enthusiasm for the enterprise. When people (i.e., teaching staff, parents, the public, school boards) see evidence of change, they are more likely to support similar changes in the future. They become optimistic about the change effort.
- Attitudes. Integration means more than having positive attitudes toward people with disabilities. But positive attitudes make a profound difference to a program's chances of success. Principals can lead the way in (a) challenging age-old stereotypes about disabilities, (b) providing a good example of natural interaction between nondisabled and disabled persons, (c) examining and altering certain language such as disability labels that unnecessarily set disabled people apart from nondisabled people, and (d) by openly exploring disability-related attitudes.

3

The Front Line . . . Teachers

STANFORD J. SEARL, JR., DIANNE L. FERGUSON, AND
DOUGLAS BIKLEN

THE MYTH OF THE SUPER TEACHER

"As long as you have a good teacher, nothing else matters." We have all heard that phrase. At times it rings true. We remember great teachers in our lives, teachers who helped shape our interests and skills. But the notion that all a student needs is a good teacher is false. And, for reasons we will discuss, the notion that a great or good teacher can somehow provide a quality education in any setting, in other words, in a "bad school" as well as a "good one," is also not true.

It is as commonplace today as it was five and six decades ago to complain about the quality of teaching and the skills of teachers. All too often, critiques of schools focus on the abilities of teachers and ignore or downplay the well-known fact that teachers, like workers or professionals in any organizational setting, tend to be more or less productive and effective depending on a broad range of factors in and outside of their organizational setting. That people, teachers included, work harder when they feel rewarded for their work should surprise no one. That teachers and their students excel when they feel part of a common mission, where they share goals and means of reaching these goals, and where they consistently talk about problems and solutions, also should not surprise us. After all, these principles apply to nearly any human organization. These and many other basic principles which we will examine influence teachers' performance.

While we did find examples of energetic and unusually talented teachers effectively integrating students with disabilities into regular public schools, sometimes almost in spite of the other staff in the building, such situations seemed problematic. These teachers are likely cases for future "burnout." In these instances, teachers found it necessary to secure support from people outside the school building; they tended not to have many friends in the school (after all, they were rule breakers); they usually worked abnormally long hours; they often provided their own supplies and other resources for their work; they felt isolated; and despite the feelings of accomplishment they saw in their students' progress, they felt as if they were fighting a losing battle or, at best, were caught in a standoff.

As we discussed in chapter one, mainstreaming may take several forms. We summarized four principal types: (1) teacher deals (this is the model in which we most often find the "super teacher"); (2) islands in the mainstream; (3) dual systems; and (4) unconditional integration. We find the most hope in this last type, for it is here that teachers have the chance of finding conditions that promote their work and, therefore, promote them. In other words, an effective teaching program works best when certain conditions are present in its formulation. Our own observations of integration efforts confirm and expand upon what educational researchers have found as the conditions most often associated with effective schooling. The following factors are generally associated with effective schools and, therefore, effective teaching.[1]

- Students are more likely to succeed in schools where teachers, teacher initiative, and teacher creativity are valued, supported, and rewarded.
- Teachers who can organize learning activities sequentially achieve more success with their students than those who cannot.
- Students learn more in classrooms where teachers are prepared, have planned their lessons, and are able to present their material in a logical fashion.

---

[1] The literature on factors or strategies that grace effective schools is extensive. For excellent reviews of this literature, see, for example, the following: D. E. Mackenzie, "Research for school improvement: An appraisal of some recent trends," *Educational Researcher*, April 1983, pp. 5–17; and M. Rutter, B. Maugham, P. Mortimore, J. Ouston, and A. Smith, *Fifteen thousand hours: Secondary schools and their effects on children* (New York: Wiley, 1975).

- Teachers need to be able to maintain group interest and to sense when group interest is waning. Students do well when, as a group, they feel involved.
- Teachers and schools that adopt and communicate common, organized, and sequential goals enable their students to progress better than those that do not. A sense of community ensues when teachers and administrators collaborate in curriculum development, problem solving, inservice training, and program development.
- Schools that emphasize success in academic and vocational areas related to success in later life tend to have more serious involvement by students.
- Many students perform better when they feel recognized, encouraged, and monitored. Whether through grading, teacher comments in class, parent/teacher conferences, daily rewards, verbal praise or some other reward, students respond to praise and concern. Even critical concern elicits student progress if meted out fairly.
- Similarly, teachers perform more effectively when they feel that someone cares about their ideas, their progress, and their contribution to the school setting. Teachers particularly welcome support and recognition from administrators and from parents.
- Teachers who interact with, and maintain a sense of, the class as a group tend to have better results than those who deal well only with individuals or very small groups of students.
- Schools and classes that emphasize and promote cooperation among students achieve greater overall success among students. Where certain groups are made to feel as outsiders and possibly less competent (e.g., girls in computer class) these students perform less well.
- Students do better when encouraged rather than browbeaten. Many students respond well to praise. Schools that use discipline judiciously appear to have fewer behavior problems. But when teachers or school administrators ignore rule infractions and other problem behaviors, the problems multiply.
- When teachers and school policies expect students to take care of their books and other classroom materials, students seem more serious about, and successful with, their work.
- Students feel more committed to the school as a group setting, and to its rules and expectations, when they remain a part of the school and its student body over several years. This supports the notion of continuity of school placements.

- Schools that hold higher expectations for student performance and expect more work of students (in class and in homework) have better records of student achievement.
- Schools that value the students (e.g., by giving them a voice in student affairs, by encouraging participation in extracurricular activities, by displaying student work) have more productive students.
- "Really" small classes that enable teachers to work more closely with individual students may help students progress.
- Smaller schools have more after-school involvement of students. Recent studies of school effectiveness (e.g., Goodlad, 1984) associate smaller schools with greater school success.
- Teachers who are able to manage several activities simultaneously (e.g., reading lesson for one group of students; involvement of other groups in independent learning activities that have been previously organized for students) enable their students to learn more effectively.
- When teachers minimize noninstructional time and other "down-time," students learn more. By the same token, increased direct instruction of students yields more learning. And when students attend school regularly they do better.
- When teachers demonstrate concern for students as people (by helping them with their problems, by listening to them, by sharing feelings with them), students tend to work harder and to show more interest in the material the teacher wishes them to master.
- When teachers model cooperative problem-solving behaviors, their students can be expected to learn from their example. Similarly, if teachers try to avoid problems, blame others for problems, or accept failure easily, then students will do the same. If teachers and administrators reveal prejudice through their own behavior, however unwittingly, students will learn these same prejudices.
- Students perform best when they know what the expectations of teachers and administrators are and when there seems to be a unity of expectations in the school setting. When students receive mixed messages (disparate goals, conflicting curricular approaches), they may feel frustrated and regard the school as working against them.
- All students tend to do better when they participate in heterogeneous school groupings than when segregated by ability.
- Students do better in systems that monitor their progress on material learned in class. Here we refer to the concept of criterion-referenced

evaluation. Assessments that are not closely related to classroom curriculum cannot have the same positive effect on student performance.
- Students do better in schools where the principal or another administrator sets high standards of achievement, communicates a commitment
to excellence, and encourages excellence among all students, irrespective of their ability level.
- Students do better in schools where principals spend at least some time
in classrooms and demonstrate a knowledge and interest in classroom
life.
- Teachers perform well when provided opportunities for independence
in their classrooms, to modify and supplement curricula, to be creative
within the overall goals of the school.
- Students who would be likely targets of prejudice and discrimination
(e.g., disabled students, black students, girls) perform better in school
environments where equality is valued, where prejudice is talked about
and criticized, where issues of differences are neither glossed over nor
unnecessarily highlighted.
- Minority students perform better in environments where they regularly
see minority role models. Nonminority students develop more positive
attitudes toward minority students when they have minority faculty
members.

In addition to these factors for success, our research identified principles that either parallel the "effective schools" items or extend them.
These relate specifically to special education, but also could apply to
"regular education":

1. The principle of integrating disabled and nondisabled students in
   the broadest possible range of events and activities
2. The principle of functional programming
3. The principle of community-referenced instruction

In this chapter we discuss the three major principles as well as numerous
subprinciples or strategies. These principles help explain the role that
teachers, preferably groups of teachers, play in making integration work.
We have consistently avoided implying that any individual teacher can
independently make integration succeed, for we think such cases are rare

and have been fraught with difficulties. These principles are best adopted by teachers in school systems that have an interest in, or some potential for, trying integration as a schoolwide or, better yet, systemwide effort. This is not to say that teachers do not matter or that teachers need not be competent, but only that teachers perform best when they work in a supportive community with common goals rather than in isolation from one another.

That teachers want information to help them mainstream effectively is indisputable. Note the following teacher comments as an example:

I don't mind having the kids in my classes. The only thing that bothers me is that I don't know what to do with them. Most of them are dyslexic, right? And we don't know how to deal with a dyslexic kid. I'm not sure Jack knows. We had this workshop on LD kids, and what it mainly seemed to tell us was how to identify an LD kid, and, once we identified them, to be patient with them, but it didn't tell us anything about how to teach them. That's what I think we need, some workshops telling us how we can teach the kids we've got in our classes.

All my past training led me to believe that mainstreaming was for physically handicapped students. Now I get LD and ED students, and it's very difficult to find materials and time to be able to really provide for them. I'm not trained for it and it's very hard to deal with them.

We also found, however, that those teachers who were most vocal in their complaints that they were "not prepared" did not always take help or training when it was offered. We did find that those teachers who had a record of willingness to experiment, to be involved in change (e.g., in open classrooms, the "new math," racial desegregation) were most likely to take advantage of training and consultation when offered.

In this chapter we describe principles and strategies we believe teachers will find useful. After talking with hundreds of teachers, observing in dozens of classroom and community sites, and reading the recent literature about teachers and teaching, we were struck by a number of underlying "principles of curriculum" for educating students with disabilities. These proposed curriculum principles bring new answers to the conventional curriculum questions, "What do I teach?" and "How do students learn?" and "How can my teaching be most effective?"

THE PRINCIPLE OF INTEGRATION

The principle applies equally well to more severely handicapped students as it does to mildly disabled students. This principle has a number of subparts, including the following:

- Integration can promote positive attitudes about students with disabilities. But to accomplish positive attitudes, they must be encouraged.
- The term *integration* applies to structured as well as unstructured social integration between typical students and those students with handicaps; programs can promote such interactions between typical and handicapped students by using such strategies as peer tutoring, special friends, and other techniques.
- Schools that value integration generally recognize the power and importance of changing attitudes on the part of everyone involved in the students' education; they consciously emphasize this aspect of the integration principle.
- Integration requires sensitivity to, and flexibility about, a variety of age-appropriate programming features, including curriculum materials and settings, and groupings that are chronologically age-appropriate.
- "Real" or "natural" mainstreaming demands dispersal of handicapped students throughout various school and community settings in approximately natural proportions; this means that if, for example, about 1 percent of the population is characterized as severely handicapped, then a school or class or community setting should also reflect that broad ratio.
- Integration may mean settling for partial participation of handicapped students with their typical peers; even if, for whatever reason, handicapped students cannot participate with their typical peers on exactly the same basis (whether physical, emotional, or mental), partial participation should be encouraged and developed by teachers.

Attitudes and Integration

What occurs when one teacher mainstreams three different students with relatively mild disabilities into her classroom? One observer described this teacher's classroom as "like an old-time sweatshop, all that goes on there is work." Signs on the door indicated problems and assignments for individual students; worksheets were piled at the edge of her desk.

Glancing about the room, one noticed project materials and displays arranged neatly, making semipartitions in some instances. The children worked at their desks, completing math problems that were written on the board; additional, individual assignment sheets had been prepared in folders for each student and left near the door. The observer cannot identify any handicapped students; they are part of the group but are not distinguishable by their handicaps.

Sharply and quickly, the teacher responded to student questions and made simple suggestions about the work, ranging from "Nancy, just keep at it for a few more minutes and I'll help," or "Of course you can do it, Kyle . . . remember how you solved it yesterday?" Even though most students worked individually for this section of the day, some had questions; a couple of times, as many as five students clustered around the teacher's desk, saying they couldn't get it, wanting the teacher to help them do the problem, chatting. Mrs. O'Day cajoled this one, teased that one, mimicked another ("Oh, look at me, I just can't do it; you poor thing"), and peppered other students with questions and comments.

Which child was handicapped? Maybe it was the student whose eyes wandered and who nodded, vaguely, toward Mrs. O'Day when she said, "Timmy, get that head down and do it; they're the same problems as yesterday."

Or could it be the girl in the front row of desks, away from the door, who doodled with her pencil as if to make little roads that snaked down to the floor?

Yet, aside from occasional snickers and daydreaming, nearly all of the almost thirty students appeared to do the math worksheets, mostly by themselves with periodic breaks to see the teacher or go to the bathroom.

After class, we sat around with Mrs. O'Day and talked. The fifth-grade teacher drummed her pencil, smiling out from behind her desk.

"People are afraid of change . . . doesn't matter if you're a teacher or what. Change bothers people and they just don't like it!"

Mrs. O'Day indicated that next year would be her twentieth year teaching elementary school, mostly fourth and fifth grade.

"I went through a lot," she said. "It was painful for me at first; the handicapped kids were so different and they made me change."

"If you can open people's heads to seeing that kids are the same whether they're deaf, blind, or purple, it's half the battle. But we've got to keep plugging at our teachers. They're scared that they're going to look like failures. You've got to show them that these kids are not THOSE kids but OUR kids. This can't be one year on, one year off. There has got to be regular inservice."

Mrs. O'Day had three students with disabilities in her regular fifth-grade class. She was clear about what worked for her mainstreamed students.

"The main thing I think is most important is I don't treat the handicapped kids any differently from any other kid."

Her hands gestured around the room, pointing to empty desks and calling up the children for us. Her voice changed, more confidential, lowered as if someone might be spying on us there in her classroom. Drawing us to a couple of wall charts, she told about how important it really was to minimize a student's handicap or disability.

"Sure, these kids may have lots of needs—speech therapy, occupational therapy, special tutors, or whatever—but we have to struggle to see them *not* as handicapped children but as kids."

In the case of Mrs. O'Day's classroom, she took three students with different labels (learning-disabled, speech-impaired, and behaviorally disordered) and found ways to include them as part of the class, irrespective of label.

Among the many strategies, Mrs. O'Day used the following:

1. By working closely with special education consultants, she knew the capabilities of all three students. Therefore, she could individualize instruction, and she could do it in the context of the larger classroom setting.
2. According to her, the biggest change was to see them as "her kids," as part of the class. "I make a lot of demands on them at times; it didn't always work, but it made a difference to the other, more typical kids."

We heard the same message across the United States: EDUCATION FOR HANDICAPPED KIDS HAS MORE TO DO WITH HOW PEOPLE *FEEL* AND *THINK* THAN ANYTHING ELSE.

We heard versions of that message again and again: *people's attitudes make a great difference*. In this case, "Don't treat the handicapped kids any differently" did not mean doing nothing; it meant using strategies to help them fit in.

Socializing

Integration brings together disabled and nondisabled students. But it does not guarantee meaningful integration. In Europe, it is common to view integration in stages: physical integration, functional integration, and social integration. Physical integration refers to the placement of students with disabilities in regular schools. Functional integration refers to programmatic integration—for example, having students with hearing problems attend regular classes where they partake of the same curriculum, albeit with the assistance of phonic ears or other technologies. Social integration refers to students learning to relate to each other as associates or friends. Here are some examples, all of which are drawn from a single classroom in an elementary school and describe the nondisabled students interacting with each other:

Hans enters the room, walks to his desk, then to Ellen's in the row behind him. He leans on Ellen's desk, looking at her paper. She continues writing, looks up at him, and smiles.

On line outside the gym, Justin, Ethan, and Drew are talking together. Justin turns to Ethan and says, "You're a pretty smart kid."

Kurt, who joins this class for lunch, enters the classroom. Adam calls to him immediately, "Sit next to me today." Kurt says, "Okay." Adam gets up and says, "I'll help you with the desk." Together, they move a desk next to Adam's desk.

They seek and provide information or assistance.

Karen Fosse (the teacher) asks Leigh to close the classroom door. After several unsuccessful attempts, Leigh approaches Woody, whose seat is closest to the door. With her finger in her mouth, she says, "Woody, how do you close the door?" Her tone is high-pitched and soft. Woody gets up from his desk, walks to the door, steps on the flat lever just underneath the cylinder, and the door swings shut. Leigh watches, with her finger in her mouth. When the door closes, Woody turns, looks at Leigh, and goes back to his seat. Leigh watches until the door is fully closed. Then, she turns and walks back to her desk. She sits down and continues working.

Adam discovers that he had made an error when called to the chalkboard during a lesson. He whispers to Ethan, sitting behind him, "Why didn't you tell me?" Ethan whispers back, "I did."

The assignment is to write each of several words listed on the board in a sentence. Judy helps the two boys on either side of her (Floyd and Garrett) sound out the letters of the words they want to write.

On occasion, the children approach each other to borrow something, or to share materials.

Ted walks over to Eileen's desk. He asks her, "Can I have some glue?" Eileen looks at him and nods. She reaches into her desk, pulls out her egg carton container, and hands Ted her small bottle of glue. Ted says, "Thanks." He walks back to his desk.

Ethan says to Ellen, "Do you have a black crayon?" Ellen replies, "Yes. In my desk. Put it back." She returns to the group in the back of the room.

Holly and Ellen are both washing their desks. Holly looks at Ellen, her eyes open wide. She says excitedly, "Do you want to trade sponges?" Ellen looks at the sponge in her hand, then she holds it out to Holly. Floyd watches them, twirling his pencil in his fingers.

Frequently, the children talk about their school work or an activity they are doing, or things in general.

While Greta washes her desk, Chad, who sits next to her, says, "Greta, I'm getting really good at that last paper. Because C starts my first name and my last name. That was a C paper." Chad is smiling. Greta smiles at him as she continues to wash her desk.

Ethan returns to his desk after reading group. He has a new reading book. Ellen says, "Adam's not in a book yet. They're not in a book yet." Adam, sitting at his desk, shakes his head. Ellen continues, "We're in 'Chug Chug.' " Ethan replies, "We're in 'Yes Yes.' " Ethan opens his book to the first page. He looks down a list of the books on the inside of the front cover. He finds "Yes Yes." Ethan says, "That's number 17. We only have three more." Then he looks up the list and locates "Chug Chug." He says, " 'Chug Chug' is number 7." Ellen nods.

Ellen, Ethan, and Holly are talking about the birds they see in their yards. Ellen says, "We feed them bird seeds." Ethan says, "That must be what they grow out of." He laughs heartily. Ellen and Holly laugh too.

Ethan, Justin, and Bert are standing next to Drew. They are talking about eating clay. Ethan says, "I ate clay." Justin says, "Here, eat some now." Ethan replies, "No, I got sick." His voice elevates in pitch. They all laugh.

During playtime each day, the students engage in a variety of activities including painting and other crafts, doing puzzles, playing checkers and other games, and playing with toys they bring from home. Throughout this period, they interact with each other freely, discussing a broad range of topics, such as the rules and strategies of the games they are playing, what they are building or creating, what is going on at home, and so forth.

For the most part, peer interactions in this class are positive. On occasion, however, a few of the children participate in more negative encounters:

Ellen begins to wash her desk. Floyd, sitting in the row behind her, says, "Can I borrow your yellow to do all this?" He points to his paper. Ellen replies, sharply, "No. I'm not sharing. And you can't have Holly's either. She only shares with me and Eileen."

Hans stands in front of Holly's desk and says to her, "Holly, I'm all done." There is excitement in his voice. Ellen, who is just sitting down at her desk, directly in front of Holly's, says sternly, making a face, "So what, Hans?" She sits down. Holly does not say anything.

The teacher would very much like Faye, a student with a disability, to interact more socially with the other students. Our observer reported that Faye typically spends a very small percentage of her time in direct contact with other children.

Overall, the children in this class are involved on a consistent basis in social interaction with their classmates. However, even though Faye spends most of each school day with the class, she is not a part of the "social life" of the class, and her interactions with her classmates are significantly different from their interactions with each other.

With the exception of one child, Leigh, who was described by her teacher as "withdrawn," Faye's classmates spend very high percentages of time in contact with each other. Even Garrett, a child who is described by the teacher as "very quiet," experiences substantially higher levels of peer involvement than does Faye, thus suggesting that her experience is indeed atypical for this setting.

Although Faye is with this class for most of the day and moves freely around the classroom, she spends much of her time alone. She completes her few assignments, and then chooses successive activities from various places around the classroom, working on each for short periods of time. Faye leaves the class regularly in the morning and the afternoon for her scheduled speech and resource programs. Ms. Fosse reminds Faye each day when it is time for her to go. Faye appears content in class yet does not object to leaving the class. Her leaving, however, occasionally deprives her of positive group experiences. She frequently misses opportunities to simply "hang out" with other students in the class because at these times she goes to the resource program.

There seems to be considerable curiosity about Faye among the other children in her class. Although they do not ask questions directly, the children frequently stare at her, particularly at her face. It is difficult to ascertain the precise nature of her classmates' curiosity. However, the staring phenomenon is a reasonable indication that curiosity does exist. In addition, Faye is, on occasion, the topic of secret conversation.

Faye is sitting at her desk. Justin is near the window, putting something in a large plastic bag, which is on the floor. Chad is standing near his desk, talking softly to Justin. Floyd is standing against the window shelf, near both Chad and Justin. As I move closer, I hear Chad say, "She's retarded." His tone is straightforward and descriptive, although he is whispering. Floyd stares at Faye. Chad looks at her over her shoulder and Justin glances over. I place my chair next to the movable shelf near the windows. I nonchalantly glance around the room. The boys stop talking and Floyd and Justin return to their seats.

Faye seldom initiates interactions of any kind with the majority of children, and she rarely communicates verbally with them, even when asked a question directly.

Faye has just finished saying that her brother played a game in her room. It is "sharing time." The children sit in a group. Hans asks Faye, "What was he playing?" There is no answer. Afterwards, Ms. Fosse says, "I'm sorry, Hans. You asked Faye a question and I didn't give her a chance to answer." Ms. Fosse repeats Hans's question to Faye. Faye says something. It is inaudible. Ms. Fosse does not elaborate.

Karen Fosse describes Faye as "doing a little better than before" but "still not communicating well."

Ms. Fosse says, "Well, she's very difficult to understand. She doesn't really initiate any conversation. She might be playing with someone and they're working together but they don't talk. She smiles all the time. Her talking is mostly one word or two words. Except when it's about her family. The other kids get tired of that."

When Faye does initiate verbalizations, they are usually directed to an adult, particularly Ms. Fosse, but frequently are unrelated to the topic under consideration.

Ms. Fosse instructs the children concerning the morning's assignments. Ms. Fosse starts walking toward the counter on the door side of the room. Faye raises her hand. Ms. Fosse stops near the door, looks at Faye, and says, "Yes, Faye." In a very unclear voice, Faye says, "It Jody birthday." Ms. Fosse says, "It's Jody's birthday? Oh, he must be very happy. Is he five or six?" Faye says, "Five." Ms. Fosse nods. Faye smiles. Greta turns around and stares at Faye.

The children in this class respond to Faye in a variety of ways, which for the most part are unlike the ways they interact with each other. With Faye, they do not exchange greetings or pleasantries, ask for or freely give assistance, share their materials, or discuss their schoolwork and other matters—as they do with each other. Many children simply look at her and back away if she gets too close. This happens while the children are standing on line, during playtime, or during a class activity. Frequently, children seem unable or unwilling to communicate directly with Faye and require the teacher to do so for them.

One of the assignments involves coloring, cutting, and pasting, in that order. Faye takes the worksheet, a blank sheet of paper, and a pair of scissors. Ted is standing near her at the counter. As she takes these items, he says, "Faye." His tone of voice is high; he looks sternly at Faye. Faye returns to her seat. Ted follows her. Faye sits down. Karen Fosse is nearby talking with another child. Ted stops next to Faye's desk in the middle aisle. He looks from Faye to Ms. Fosse a few times. He has a worried look on his face. Ms. Fosse turns around, walks toward the center aisle, and stops next to Faye. She says calmly to Faye, "First color all the pictures before you cut." Ms. Fosse takes the scissors to the holder on the counter. Ted returns to his seat.

Faye also experiences more directly negative encounters with her classmates. These include such things as unpleasant facial expressions toward her, mocking, overt rejection, and other negative acts.

Ellen primarily, and her friend, Holly, interact with Faye most consistently. Ellen occupies the desk adjacent to Faye's and Holly sits directly behind Ellen. The behavior of both girls toward Faye is characterized more by authoritativeness than by egalitarianism. Both attempt to direct her, control her, keep her in line.

At about 12:00 p.m., Holly and Greta look at the clock, then over to Faye, who is still eating her lunch. Holly says loudly and strongly, "Food, out." She points toward the door. Greta stands with her looking at Faye.

Ellen is chosen with another girl to push the tray cart to the cafeteria. Just before she leaves, she says, "Don't let her touch my desk." She is talking to Holly in a firm, almost bitter tone. When Ellen returns from pushing the cart, the first thing she does is ask Holly, "Did Faye touch my desk?" Holly replies, "No," and shakes her head.

On the way back to her desk, Faye walks past Floyd's desk and touches the elf he has made. Floyd is in the "Thunderbirds" reading group, now in session. Holly, who is sitting next to Floyd's desk, frowns at Faye, grabs Floyd's elf and says sternly, "Don't touch."

Faye is not always a passive bystander in these encounters. Her reputation for having "sticky fingers" and Ellen's belongings being frequently the target have not facilitated the development of a trusting, equal relationship. Frequently, however, Faye pursues Ellen, without much success.

Faye sits down on the floor near Ellen. Ellen pushes herself backward, away from the group.

Ellen is moving her desk away from Faye's toward Adam's. Faye follows Ellen's movements, by moving her own desk in the same way.

When the observer reported to the teacher that Ellen and Holly interact with Faye more than the other children do, and that their interactions consist mainly of reprimanding her or giving her instructions or directions, Ms. Fosse nodded her head and replied, "They think they are helping her. Now, Judy and Leigh play with her." However, on no occasion were either Judy or Leigh observed playing with Faye.

In fact, on only one occasion was Faye observed actually playing with any other child. Justin and Faye were "water painting" over each other's chalk drawings on a slate easel near the back of the classroom.

This activity, however, was abruptly interrupted when Faye was told to leave the classroom for speech.

Karen Fosse reported only one other incident where a child, Bert, attempted to relate to Faye in a play activity. According to Ms. Fosse, Faye and Bert were sitting at the puzzle table in the back of the room. Bert tried to engage Faye in a conversation but was unsuccessful. "She gave him no response at all. Not one word or anything. And Bert has always been very kind to her."

There is no doubt that Karen Fosse is concerned about Faye—about her interactions with the other children, her abilities to communicate with them, and the appropriateness of her even being in this class. This concern, however, seems to be expressed in two characteristic and somewhat conflicting ways. On the one hand, Karen Fosse and, indeed, Mary Engel, the lunch aide, are overprotective of Faye, hurrying to do for her what she can do for herself or could ask a peer to do, and to excuse, in subtle ways, important deviations from standard rules of behavior. On the other hand, Faye's success with her peers seems to be left entirely up to her. Karen Fosse herself wonders if Faye should be in this group if she is unable to communicate with her peers. Little specific intervention is offered to facilitate positive interactions with Faye. The only possible exception is a discussion about Faye in her absence which was reported by the teacher. It is difficult to determine the result of this discussion, since no change in the children's behavior was noted by the observer.

In the course of our observations we noted this type of noninteraction or relative isolation as typical of situations where teachers had not actively intervened to create alternative patterns of interactions. One interpretation of Faye's situation is that she is a lonely person, "that's her personality." Another is that she lacks interactive skills, something that we can help her develop. Another is that her nondisabled peers simply do not want to relate to her, they have a more natural affinity for each other. We regard none of these explanations as satisfactory. We can no more accept these explanations than we can accept the notion that black or white students have a "natural" affinity for other students of their own color. Such grouping by character trait reflects socialization. It is learned behavior. If nondisabled students have not learned how to interact with a student who has a disability, of course it will be difficult; if they do learn these skills, then they will likely display them. Similarly, if we expect interaction skills from disabled students, we must teach them those skills. In a setting where the formal and informal curriculum included socializing, we observed students who knew how to interact with other disabled and nondisabled students. We observed students who knew how to talk about their disabled peers in positive ways. For example, such a student remarked:

> Peter gets so excited sometimes that he has a hard time saying what he means. I just wait for him. That's the way he is.
> Jack likes to go to the gym. I do too. I sometimes get to go to the gym with him. We play games and stuff. We take turns bouncing a ball around.
> Mary can't talk. But she knows some signs. Her teacher teaches us signs too.

This student is the same age as Faye's peers. She attends a class in which students are encouraged to learn about differences and to socialize with each other in a variety of ways. In another school, we observed that a teacher identified those activities in which a disabled student had great interest and facility (e.g., a mildly autistic youngster liked to work on computer word games) and then used these activities as contexts for encouraging student cooperation and integration.

Teacher Modeling

One obvious way that teachers can promote social interaction of disabled and nondisabled students is by modeling that interaction themselves. This helps nondisabled students learn what is possible. If a nondisabled student observes a teacher telling a joke to a disabled student or listening interestedly to a disabled student's story, then the nondisabled student can begin to learn that skill. If a teacher fails to respond to a severely disabled student, either verbally or in action, nondisabled students will learn that not to respond is appropriate. If, on the other hand, the teacher uses sign language with a student or works with a student to verbalize correctly, then other students will begin to emulate the teacher, particularly if they are encouraged to do so. In the first chapter of this book, we provided a case in point. A parent was quoted as saying,

> My child can talk. And, that's one reason why he can. It's because of the other children. The typical children kept coming up to him and talking to him and demanding that he talk. They knew how to get an answer from him and they wouldn't let him get away with a single-syllable response. Now I ask

you, what teacher or teachers could do that for my son, much less for a whole class of kids with autism? That's just not realistic.

In this instance the teacher had demonstrated how nondisabled students could interact with a disabled student verbally. The nondisabled students learned from this and helped their disabled peer develop his language.

In another instance we observed a gym teacher working well with a severely retarded junior high student. He helped the student develop gross motor coordination. He spoke to the other students as well as to the other teacher, telling them that the disabled student understood much more than he could communicate. This realization helped the teacher and the students adjust their own way of interacting with the disabled student so that they were not talking to him as if he were a baby or as if he could not comprehend what they were saying. Students learned that their disabled peer could appreciate a sense of humor for example. In other instances we observed that the potential for teachers to serve as models for the nondisabled students was lost simply because the teachers did not capitalize on opportunities for creating student-to-student interaction. In this next example, Susan is a teacher assistant and Jerry is a severely physically disabled fourth-grade student with cerebral palsy who uses a communication board to communicate. Jerry attends a regular fourth-grade class:

Jerry was completing four or five pages out of his workbook. These were pages the other students were working on as well. He read a sentence and then pointed to the word that he wanted in the space. Susan then wrote in the word. At one point he had made a mistake and wanted the words changed. With little confusion, Susan knew what needed to be done. She erased what was already in the space. They seemed to understand one another. Susan told us that she strongly believes Jerry needs to do his schoolwork on his own. Periodically, she prods him on with "Listen to this," and "Pay attention, 'cause this is important to get." When Jerry first entered the class, he needed everything done for him. But, after developing work contracts and making him do for himself, Susan continues to try not to intervene too much.

How could interaction be encouraged for Jerry? The teachers could schedule times and activities when nondisabled students could team up with Jerry. The teacher could teach nondisabled students how to use Jerry's communication board and, more specifically, how to develop language entries for the board. This could aid them in interacting with Jerry.

The teachers could teach about differences as part of the curriculum; they could, for example, invite an adult with cerebral palsy to make a presentation to the class about his or her life, job, aspirations, and experiences.

An art teacher with whom one researcher spoke had made social interaction a part of the entire classroom motif: "I set up peer helpers among all kids, not just special ed. This sets up camaraderie, fosters acceptance. Also, there's more mobility in the art room. I see kids sitting together, talking together." Other teachers speak of adapting their teaching styles as a means of achieving a positive academic learning environment *and* promoting an ethic of inclusion rather than a message, however unconscious, of exclusion. An English teacher describes her adaptation in teaching style as a result of mainstreaming: "I am more oral in my presentations and evaluations now. I find that this is easier to monitor the program for all kids, and then I don't have to send the special ed. kids out and back to their rooms for help."

The following are practical strategies for promoting interaction between disabled and nondisabled students.

1. Disperse students with disabilities into groups of nondisabled students. In other words, avoid congregation of students with disabilities.
2. Integrate support services such as speech therapy, remediation in reading and math, and other resource help into the regular classroom setting.
3. Teachers can serve as models of how to interact with disabled students.
4. Teach about differences as part of the regular curriculum.
5. Structure social interaction in the classroom through planned activities (e.g., role playing, biographical interviews, group projects, student reviews of each others' work).
6. Teach nondisabled students about aids that are useful to disabled students (e.g., communication boards, wheelchairs, sign language).
7. Ensure, as much as possible, that students with disabilities follow the same or similar patterns of classroom and schoolwide activity scheduling as nondisabled students.
8. Avoid references to, and language about, students with disabilities that might set them apart from the rest of the class (e.g.,

references to "our CP kids," or use of nicknames for disabled
students but not for others).

9. Where individualization is necessary for mainstreamed students,
   attempt to have it occur when other students are receiving individualized instruction.

10. Comment positively on social interaction between disabled and
    nondisabled students.

Some educators might ask, "Is it legitimate to teach socializing as
part of the curriculum? Isn't it better for kids to develop this on their
own, to pursue their own interests in terms of friends?" Clearly, we must
answer "No." Selma Greenberg has noted that at the age of three, boys
and girls in daycare programs already display sex-stereotyped interests.
Girls play with dolls. Boys play with blocks. Girls avoid competitive
outdoor games. Girls like to play with clothes. Boys don't play with
clothes. And so it goes, boys playing with other boys at one set of
particular activities, girls playing with girls at other types of activities.
At a later age, girls are more likely to concentrate in subjects such as
home economics, typing, and literature, while boys are more likely to
pursue auto mechanics, engineering, and mathematics. If educators do
not intervene at an early age, then a whole range of activities and interactive experiences are lost to both boys and girls. In effect, if we fail to
intervene, we submit students to lower quality social and academic education than we are capable of providing to them. Similarly, if we fail to
intervene with disabled and nondisabled students, we acquiesce to a lower
quality of education for both disabled and nondisabled students. The point
is, if we want integration we must structure it.

Traditionally, teachers argue for segregating more severely handicapped students from regular education settings. Teachers may feel that
because of special needs and specialized services, the more severely
handicapped students need a special environment, distinct and separate
from more typical students. Thus, today, many students with more severe
handicaps remain in separate, segregated private or public settings. Yet,
many teachers, as well as districts, regions, and states, have found ways
to change these practices of separate, segregated education for more
severely handicapped students while maintaining a high quality of necessary specialized services.

Further, teachers discovered that mainstreaming itself offers many
possibilities not available in more restricted, separate settings. The social

aspects of integrated education cannot—literally—be matched by traditional exclusion. Teachers builld upon social interaction and make special friendships, pairings, and tutoring a part of the basic curriculum.

None of the following strategies and stories can be available to teachers in *separate educational* settings.

Nonhandicapped Helpers and Peer Tutors

In a number of different contexts and classrooms, many schools have nondisabled students working together with severely handicapped children. In classes with a number of severely handicapped students, the nondisabled peers may help with instruction. Or a nondisabled student may act as a tutor, helping a severely disabled student learn to use a record player or to play a computer game. Such activities can be entered into cooperatively by disabled and nondisabled students.

In other instances, nondisabled students pair with handicapped children more informally, simply as companions and friends. They come into the classroom at either lunchtime or activity time or in another context. They play together, sit together at lunch, or go through the lunch line together. A student in an adaptive wheelchair is pushed to the lunchroom by a nondisabled third-grader. Once inside the gym/lunchroom, they make their way through the line; the student with disabilities carries her own tray, but is pushed by the nondisabled student. They sit in the midst of the noisy, boisterous students at one of the long tables. The nondisabled student helps with the adaptive spoon and puts the straw in the milk carton for the student with disabilities. Otherwise they sit together and the nondisabled student asks how things are going and whether Mary likes the lunch; the answer is usually a nod or eye contact.

Special Friend Program

In an elementary school in the Northeast, fifth-grade students enter the classroom and sign a piece of paper hanging near the door and join their special friends in whatever activity is going on. One fifth-grade girl sets up objects for Katie to move to on her scooter board and pick up, as a way of helping her learn the names of the objects. Another student joins Terry who extends her arm in order to activate a special switch that operates a tape recorder. As the tape stops, the fifth-grader talks to Terry about "making more music" so they can sing together. One student meets her Special Friend at the door of the school and walks with her to the classroom, chatting and encouraging her not to let the walker bump into walls.

As a part of one Special Friend program, fourth- and fifth-graders spend about thirty minutes a day for three-week rotations getting to know and help a student with disabilities. At the beginning, each Special Friend signs a contract that states: "I, _____, promise to do my best as a Special Friend. I will be sure that being a Special Friend does not interfere with my classroom work."

At first, staff spend time with each Special Friend; they introduce them to a student with disabilities and help them decide what they would like to do together. At the end of a three-week period the principal presents each Special Friend with a certificate during the fourth and fifth lunch period and thanks them for their participation. Some of the Special Friends explain their interest in the program this way: "It helps me learn more patience." "I like to see people happy." "My mother teaches a special class and I want to see what it is like." "It's fun." "I want to help other kids learn." While such comments suggest that the Special Friend program may reinforce the notion that disabled students always need help and are essentially dependent, the hope is that the program demonstrates to non-disabled students that they can be around, work with, and even enjoy time spent with disabled students. Nondisabled students benefit from such interactions by learning to overcome their stereotyping of and prejudices about people with disabilities.

Staff express their pleasure at the reception of the Special Friend program by talking about some of their plans to expand. For example, they arrange for Don to begin spending time in a typical gym class for part of each day and are teaching some of the nondisabled students the sign language Don uses. Don already joins this class for lunch and cooking activities. As one teacher explains it, "We've spent so much time getting our program together, we just haven't explored all the possibilities for integration that this school offers."

It is, of course, imperative that using nondisabled students as helpers and tutors not be a substitute for the school's meeting its responsibility to maximize independence of disabled students by utilizing available technologies, making the building accessible, and adequately staffing a program.

Unstructured Social Interaction

A number of positive interactions occur within integrated settings. As one principal comments, many of the interactions between nondisabled and disabled students may be more beneficial to the former than to the latter. It is important to note that disabled students should not be stereotyped as totally dependent. In many situations they can be the helpers. Several examples of positive interactions follow:

1. With a severely disabled student who was placed in the typical fourth-grade classroom, a sixth-grader had made a sorting box, with soap, toothbrushes, combs, and barrettes, and would spend time every day with the sorting task. He even had his own data sheet and when the child in the adaptive chair would make noise or flail her arms in response, the sixth-grader waited and said, "No you'll have to put the comb in the box now."

2. In a classroom for the multiply handicapped, nondisabled students would pair up with disabled students. At first, the third-grade teacher (for nondisabled students) said that eating lunch together was a "big deal." Now, however, it was more routine. The nondisabled students had realized a relatively sophisticated point: just because a particular student does not talk or respond as the rest of us, one cannot assume that such a student does not care or feel. One may not know.

3. In a number of the classes, students from regular classes line up and ask if they can be the ones to wheel or push the students to lunch, recess, physical education, the bus, or other activities. Because the students with handicaps are in the regular public school setting, a wide variety of students engage in the normal social interactions of "Hi, how are you?" in a friendly, familiar, matter-of-fact way.

4. One "labeled student," who was integrated into the regular kindergarten, had a tendency to wander out of the classroom and into the halls or gym. The teacher said that many times an older student would pick up the child and return him to the classroom.

5. Another example happened with a second-grade "special" student who had a schedule that included many different changes, including a different room for art, a resource room, music, and gym. Without a prompt, a couple of her second-grade peers said, "Wait, it's not time to go to art, it's time for the music," and they took her along with

them. There was not a teacher or aide around at the moment; but the students knew the schedule anyway.

6. One boy, classified as multiply handicapped, was extremely shy and tended to isolate himself from others. In particular, he did not want to get off the school bus in the morning. The principal observed that a high-school-level student came along and convinced the boy to come into the kindergarten. Once in the room, the secondary-age student sat briefly with the student. Of course, again, such a social interaction was not planned: it happened because that is what occurs when people get together.

7. One of the more severely handicapped children had problems keeping food in her mouth because of tongue thrust and several related problems. While she was eating, a number of other children were there. One of the boys picked up a towel that was beside her and wiped her mouth off, saying, "There, you look better now."

Normalizing Language

Integration means more than mere physical integration. Ideally, it means functional (program) and social integration as well. To accomplish this goal, we need to create an *atmosphere of inclusion*. Each of the strategies described in this section speaks to this matter of inclusion, but none may be as important as the strategy we are about to advance, the strategy of normalizing language.

Special educators, like any professional group, often speak in a shorthand language that they understand but which sets them apart from other people. When a teacher speaks of "contingencies," "differential reinforcement," "self-stim behaviors," "psychoeducational," and "LRE," "FAPE" (Free Appropriate Public Education), "ED," and "SMH" only other special educators and, perhaps other related specialists, will understand his or her meaning. When we talk about education as "treatment" or instruction as "clinical programming" we convey a message that "special education" is indeed different from regular education. Inadvertently, we stigmatize the students by identifying them with something other than regular education, and something that sounds more like medical care for people who are sick or in some other way different.

In the following list we offer areas of classroom programming where teachers can and should attempt to maintain typical, nonspecial language to describe them:

1. Names for classroom and groups of students in class.
2. Terms for classroom activities (e.g., reading, domestic living skills, math, recreation, physical education, language arts, vocational education, home economics, social studies, spelling, and civics).
3. Teaching methods.
4. Curricular materials (workbooks, texts, handouts, objects).
5. Information provided on forms such as Individual Education Plans, due process notification, public notices, and so forth.
6. Correspondence between "special" and "regular" educators.
7. Correspondence between the school district and families.
8. Case materials on students.
9. All communication with the public (e.g., news articles, publications, teachers' presentations to public gatherings, etc.).
10. And names and nicknames of individual students as well as programs.

A Story of Structured Integration

"At first, they really gave it to Bennie; he simply looked different. But, it's a real problem: he can't do all of the work."

Mrs. Lake teaches a fourth-grade class in an inner-city neighborhood; a number of students with disabilities have been "mainstreamed" in the neighborhood elementary school; one particular student, with some physical involvement (who was also labeled "emotionally disturbed"), has joined Mrs. Lake's classroom.

The rules for proper behavior were clear and posted—conspicuously—in at least two different places in the classroom: STAY IN YOUR SEAT/WORK SILENTLY.

On the blackboard, printed in oversized letters, two lists of names stood out from the daily assignments and related notices:

NO LIST
The three names under this list would lose privileges or might stay after school or write 100 times, "I must not . . ."

100 CLUB
The ten students under this heading would be rewarded with special privileges.

This is a tough-minded, inner-city teacher with a no-nonsense approach to classroom management; furthermore, Mrs. Lake indicated that she keeps very close to her students outside of class. She visits all of the parents regularly and tries to understand what happens to the children in her class as well as outside of the classroom. Bennie, a child labeled "emotionally disturbed," has been part of Mrs. Lake's fourth-grade class for six months.

"Bennie goes out for resource room help every morning; otherwise, he's with all of the rest of us for reading and math. He goes with the other kids for music."

Mrs. Lake said that it was difficult for her at first with Bennie.

"You know, I run on schedule and make it my business to know how the kids really feel. With Bennie, at first . . . even for a couple of months . . . it was awful."

How so? we wondered.

"Bennie seemed fine, mostly. Once a week or so, he might get upset, frustrated at his work or something, and act up. You know, scream and have a little tantrum. But, we settled him down. It was the other kids . . . they really surprised me."

She continued, "I really make a point of knowing what's happening in my class. So I saw it immediately: a couple of boys teased Bennie, made faces at him, making fun of his tantrums, saying he was a 'creep.' Then, I saw the notes and picture. For the first time in my eight years of teaching, I didn't really know what to do. It was so unfair and ridiculous. But what should I do?"

She went on, "so I got really upset about my kids calling out and writing notes about Bennie as 'retarded' or a 'retard' or 'crazy.' We talked; I cajoled. We talked some more and the ringleaders have laid off."

Mrs. Lake said that it was particularly difficult with Bennie because, in at least some of the instances, it was difficult to tell whether some of the laughter could be ridicule or play or fun.

She rolled her eyes and pushed away from the small table in the teacher's lounge.

"You know what the biggest problem was?" We waited.

"I simply tried to do it all *by myself*."

Mrs. Lake explained that with a couple of kids who weren't as handicapped as Bennie, she would send them to the resource room or to special teachers and have done with it. But with Bennie, it was different.

The other children's reactions—with their teasing and ridicule—moved her to other actions.

"For the first time, I consulted with the resource room teacher and with the special education coordinator for the building. I mean I really talked with them—laid it out. What a difference! For the first time in ten years, other professionals came into my classroom in order to observe and help—with practical suggestions—not evaluations and ratings."

Mrs. Lake said that they all agreed: Bennie did need some positive relationships and interactions with other students, which Mrs. Lake could not provide herself. More than anything else, Bennie needed a feeling of self-confidence and a sense of connection with peers and other schoolmates.

"We have some free time during the first half hour or so after the children arrive in the morning. We thought: Why not have a sixth-grader or at least someone who was seen as older by my fourth-grade kids come in and work with Bennie on a special crafts project? I had a couple of students working on a papier-mâché castle."

She grinned and it turned into a broad smile.

"For the ridicule, it took about two weeks. With this special, older friend, my kids started to see Bennie differently. They *asked* to play with him; and it carried over to the playground during recess and after school."

With some of Bennie's reading problems, Mrs. Lake used a version of the same approach. Only this time, the special education coordinator decided to use one of their "floating" aides for three hours a week in Mrs. Lake's classroom, mainly to work on reading comprehension with Bennie. He had trouble doing the workbook exercises.

"But it's just short-term," Mrs. Lake said. "We're hoping that we can arrange with one of the sixth-grade students to take over the 'tutoring' of Bennie." Mrs. Lake put her elbows on the table and leaned over to us.

"Frankly, I have never thought much about working with other teachers in the school. But this is different. It's exciting and creative, working with the sixth-grade teacher, the special ed folks, the resource person . . . and even the principal has got involved."

Finally, Mrs. Lake made the point about Bennie that other teachers repeat: "He's real different: You can't wish away those differences either. But you try to tinker and adjust. And now the biggest things of all: You can't do it all alone. Get help. Work with others."

She pushed herself away from the table and got up.

"Who knows, you might even *like* it," she added.

Mrs. Lake did something that challenges many teachers: eventually, and under some stress, she brought other professionals into her room and got help. There were two major aspects of this assistance:

1. Mrs. Lake never tried to ignore the social interaction issues that confronted her. She did not whitewash the situation by saying "They're all just kids. They're all the same." She realized that if the students were to learn to accept *and* value each other she had to intervene.
2. The support and advice had a personal, at times emotional, dimension, also. As Mrs. Lake said, "she felt isolated and alone" and such feelings increased the frustration about how to teach Bennie *and* how to integrate him, socially, with the rest of the students in the class. The fact that she worked with the resource teacher and the special education coordinator meant that Mrs. Lake had broken the isolation of the self-contained classroom teacher. She said, "Before Bennie, I could afford to be self-sufficient, depending upon my own skills and ideas; I didn't really *need* anyone else." Mrs. Lake enjoys working with other teachers and resource people; it's fun for her and breaks the circle of isolation.

Mrs. Lake received advice, support, and assistance about particular strategies; with the resource room teacher and the special education coordinator, she brainstormed ideas. Two major suggestions were helpful and crucial: An aide came for a couple of hours a day, two to three days per week. This provided relief and a structured, one-to-one teaching opportunity with Bennie; the introduction of an older student as friend and "tutor" helped to solve the ridicule problem.

THE PRINCIPLE OF FUNCTIONAL PROGRAMMING

The struggle to educate students with disabilities has deep historical roots and most often tells a tale of failure, frustration, and fear. Students with disabilities have long been associated with, and identified by, a series of failure motifs. This association with failure makes it difficult for people to see handicapped students as valuable and important individuals—individuals who learn and grow. This association with failure has always represented the biggest challenge to teachers. In one way or

another, students with disabilities are thought not to be able to learn—
to learn enough, learn the same way or as fast—as schools and teachers
are prepared to teach.

Schools and teachers think of what they do in particular ways. They
reflect an understanding of what education means and what the curriculum
content is (and ought to be) in the ways they work every day. Understanding how students with disabilities have been integrated into our
schools involves understanding the perspectives and approaches to educational and curriculum content that teachers employ.

We found three distinctly different approaches to education and curriculum content reflected in the words, activities, and feelings of teachers
to whom we spoke. Here we will call these approaches (1) the developmental learner approach, (2) the clinical-treatment approach, and (3) the
functional life skills approach. Sometimes one or several of these
approaches encourage and facilitate integration of some students with
handicaps; at other times some approaches do not. As we describe each
approach in turn, we will examine this feature.

The Developmental Learner Approach

This is the most widespread and general approach to education and
curriculum content. Education for all students, regardless of their abilities
or disabilities, seems to begin with this approach and with its key notion:
Students learn skills and information in a predictable sequence and at a
more or less predictable rate. Students learn to crawl before they walk,
babble before they talk, talk before they read, add before they multiply.

Students with disabilities who might learn in a different order or at
a different rate are usually seen as lagging behind in a growth process.
Students are "delayed" or "behind" in development compared to the
majority of students who are the same chronological age. The teacher
guides growth in a particular sequence to help the student "catch up." It
is hoped the student will respond by acquiring new knowledge or skills,
at a faster rate. The ultimate goal is to have the student become as able
as her peers—to catch up to the norm, or at least to narrow the distance
between present performance and the norm. Sometimes even if a student
doesn't "learn faster" or "eventually catch up to the norm," adaptation
can easily be made.

For some students the approach "works." The following examples illustrate this fact:

- A student with mild cerebral palsy has trouble learning to write; the teacher arranges for some resource room help and peer tutoring. With practice and assistance, the student gets to grade level.
- Because writing is awkward and slow, a student uses a tape recorder to take notes and exams.
- A visually impaired student uses a monocular to get around the school building and see the board. The student uses large-print books, tapes, and occasionally readers, to study new material.

But for some students with disabilities, the developmental gap widens beyond the capacity of special "catch-up" sessions, adaptations, or temporary removal from the regular class for help. The removal that was originally intended to be temporary becomes permanent.

A recurring model of special education has been for teachers to use special, segregated placements outside the regular classroom setting to assist handicapped students to "catch up" to the norm. When many of the more severely handicapped students do not "catch up" and the developmental gap widens, handicapped students remain forever segregated from typical students.

Typical developmental patterns and stages represent *averages*, a composite version based upon significant individual differences. No one "fits" perfectly; furthermore, by using the developmental milestones as key indicators of student progress, the teacher may take an unfortunate, unnecessary negative view about student progress and focus upon what the student *cannot* do instead of what the student *can* perform.

In addition, teachers may experience some of the following dilemmas:

1. Many students, particularly those with disabilities, may not grow and develop in typical ways.
2. To expect typical development might place some students in categories that make it virtually impossible to learn. For example, if one of the requirements for all students is that they be toilet-trained before attending school, some students might never attend.
3. For many disabled students, deficits widen as they grow older. This can discourage and frustrate many teachers.

4. After many years with the same students in separate, segregated classes, teachers may feel hopeless about student "progress" defined in these developmental terms.

The Clinical Treatment Approach

The developmental learner approach—which dominates our public schools and encourages segregation of some handicapped students—is reinforced by another approach to education and curriculum that has come to schools from those settings more traditionally charged with serving and caring for our most severely disabled, difficult-to-teach students.

Until very recently, the education, treatment, and programming for students labeled as "severely" handicapped has been characterized by frequent segregation, institutionalization, and weak to nonexistent programming. Whatever or wherever the program, it would be dominated by a commitment to a "clinical treatment" or "therapeutic" approach. Physical and occupational therapy, as well as speech therapy, would be the key "treatments." Students would be taken to the various therapies *outside* the classroom and given individual sessions. Typically, therapists might concentrate upon range of motion, head control, balance, mouth closure. The assumption would be that once students could have better balance or hold up their heads, they would be able to pick up objects, grasp toys, or start to be able to feed themselves.

The focus would be on "improvement" or "getting better." There would be little need for handicapped youngsters to interact and mix with typical students. The focus of clinical "intervention" would be relatively narrow and specific: Get the students to pay attention, bear weight, work when sitting; and *then* they might be able to do the kinds of things that would allow them to interact "successfully" with nonhandicapped peers. To "educate" becomes to "treat deficits" and try to overcome them through regular, technical exercise or intervention. It employs a narrow, precise, and therapeutic context for learning. Of course, once the student improves (becomes less "atypical"), *then* he or she will be able to develop skills to cope in a less intensive, less segregated setting.

Teachers using this clinical treatment approach often find their role to be one of caring for students between therapy appointments. Their contribution as educators to the student's overall program is often seen as secondary to the necessary expert and technical programs provided by the therapists. Here, education means treatment. The approach originates from a medical perspective and concentrates upon overcoming "deficits."

This model, clinical treatment, is most likely to frustrate teachers and students.

1. Since it is not an educational approach per se, the teacher may have difficulty "integrating" therapy with the other program components.
2. There is a tendency to concentrate upon *eliminating* behavior and upon students' deficits.
3. The approach may imply that students "get better" or are "cured." This breeds frustration when the student is not cured.

For some students, with each passing year, the prospect for meeting the educational goal of these two approaches—overcoming the deficit or catching up to the norm—gets dimmer and dimmer. Some teachers may even begin to wonder if they are teaching anything at all. Frequently, such thoughts, even when unspoken, lead teachers of such students to feelings of fatigue, frustration, and isolation.

The developmental learner approach *does* work for some students with disabilities. But, together with the clinical treatment approach, it simultaneously encourages segregation. Teachers, perhaps better than any others, articulate the "reality" these approaches to education and curriculum content create. "It just doesn't work the way it is supposed to. Smooth transition from one developmental level to another is more a hope than reality." Or, "After all, the vast majority of these kids with the more severe disabilities are still in segregated, sometimes private, schools. It's business as usual."

Many teachers express surprise that in day-to-day classroom practice, children they know as multiply handicapped or severely and profoundly retarded are served in *quality* settings that are public and integrated with typical students.

The Functional Approach

This perspective begins by seeing the student as different, but not *too* different. The educational strategy becomes: How can we help both the student and the student's environment adapt to each other? One can accommodate differences, even very big ones, by bringing the skills the student *does* have into correspondence with the skills others have and use.

The functional life skills approach presumes that the whole community becomes the basis for this curriculum approach. Instead of simulated and preparatory activities, curricula are comprised of real-life training situations (e.g., learning to use real money rather than play money, learning to use a real bus system rather than getting on and off a model bus). This approach builds upon the things that a student *can do* and tries to adapt and adjust to take advantage of interests or skills.

1. Students with more severe disabilities become part of the community and the school.
2. Teachers and students concentrate upon those positive things that students *can do* and thus expectations can be more affirmative.
3. Through various modifications and adaptations, students focus their learning on real-world skills in the actual community settings of both the present and future.

The functional approach can only work optimally in an integrated school program. True, certain functional activities can occur in a segregated school (e.g., learning to tell time, learning to read or to communicate), but the very definition of "functional" demands integration. The functional approach builds on a student's skills, using natural events, situations, and materials, to enable a student to function as independently and effectively as possible in the mainstream of society. To take students out of the mainstream and educate them in segregated schools is to create a make-believe or at least unnatural or abnormal environment, whereas the integrated school casts disabled students into situations that are far more like the integrated life situations for which all students are being prepared.

There were two ways people talked about the kinds of activities this perspective suggests:

1. *"You find ways for a student to do those things that, if he* didn't *do them, someone else would have to."* For example, Michael cannot tell time yet. He cannot count or talk about yesterday. But he does know "time" in a functional sense: when he sees others line up for lunch, he does the same. Michael may never learn to tell time the way other children do, but he can notice certain cues around him and

react accordingly. Teachers can reinforce this attention to such cues by praising his responses.

For Michael and other students, teachers can help turn their "differences" into just different ways of doing things for themselves; for example, use snaps or velcro fasteners so no one has to zip a student's coat; or adapt doorknobs with rubber covers so that students themselves can turn them.

It is not always easy to figure out these adaptations or accommodations. Sometimes we saw whole groups of people—a teacher, a physical therapist, an adaptive physical education teacher, a parent—talking about and trying different ideas until a solution was found.

Sometimes a particular student will not be able to do something completely alone; making toast for breakfast might mean just pushing down the handle of the toaster; eating a meal might mean learning to swallow well enough so you can finish when everyone else does; getting dressed might mean being able to roll over at the proper time, or taking off the shoes someone else has already untied. Even learning to do little parts of things means that someone else doesn't have to do them for you.

Thinking about education this way seems to have helped teachers find new things to teach and students new things to learn. As one teacher said, "You don't *have* to wait until they are ready."

Robert-Andrew does not talk. He has never babbled or even gestured very clearly. But when he points to the picture of a cup on his communication board, people know he wants a drink. No one is sure that he understands that the picture is a cup, but he always drinks after pointing to the cup. Robert-Andrew's communication board only has ten pictures so far. Maybe he will learn some signs. Right now he has ten ways to tell people what he wants or does not want, even if it is without words or sentences.

2. *"You find ways for a student to do the kinds of things everyone else does."* For example, Peggy can't read and she has great difficulty turning the pages of a book; but she enjoys looking at the pages and likes to have someone read to her. Still, Peggy can go to the library with the other eight-year-olds and help to check out her own books. Certainly, Peggy would not use the library or the books in just the same way the other children do; but there would be a particular similarity—an equivalence—about the way Peggy uses the library along with the other eight-year-olds.

A principal told us, "They don't always have to be learning some specific things. It is functional just to be able to be part of the group." While we disagree with this downplaying of the importance of constant learning, we cannot argue with the benefits of integrated group experiences. Some examples might be going to a basketball game to enjoy the lights and noise, riding a bus, playing in a park, or watching airplanes. These are all ways of being part of the group.

From this functional perspective, education takes on broader meanings. In particular, we saw the education of students happening in a variety of community settings. Students learn to do parts of jobs in restaurants and hospitals, shop in grocery stores or malls, and learn to cross streets.

The teachers who talked about education this way said something else as well. In many instances old feelings of frustration and even hopelessness had been replaced by enthusiasm. Granted, teachers continue to struggle with a lot of the same questions, but they seem confident that they will create the answers. This approach seemed to work in part because it was creative. Curriculum is created every day anew in the classroom. There are no prepackaged guides or materials to use or plans to follow.

Teachers should not develop integrated, functional, and community-based curricula without really knowing the students for whom these approaches are intended. That is why we have taken the strategy of describing basic perspectives or models (e.g., functional programming, community-referenced programming) rather than trying to present "packaged" curricula. We presume that teachers can best create and adapt curricula to meet the needs of students.

As we have noted elsewhere in this chapter, teachers in successful school programs know their students well. They know their academic strengths and weaknesses; they know their interactive style; they know something about their lives outside of school; they know about their aspirations, their feelings, their fears. In most instances, teachers learn about their students informally, in the course of the year.

In one high school, we interviewed each of the students in a resource program. From these interviews we learned the importance of knowing the students in order to accomplish integrated, functional, and community-referenced programming, all of which were goals of this program. The program served twelve students. We introduce this particular classroom and its students here because we think they reveal the importance of building a functional program based on a knowledge of the students. Each of the students had a history of school failure. Almost all were held back at least once in earlier grades. By the time they entered junior high school they were all reading far below grade level. Now that they are in high school, many are reading at the third-grade level. All of the twelve have been categorized as "neurologically impaired" or "learning-disabled" (LD), though many of them might easily be labeled educable mentally retarded and several had previously been classified as emotionally disturbed.

Lou, for example, sixteen, is six-feet two-inches tall, and was diagnosed early in elementary school as having delayed speech, attributed to emotional disturbance. At one point in his schooling, he was given an intelligence test. He scored 54, at the bottom range of mild mental retardation. But just two years ago his intelligence score was 83, too high for the educable (mild) classification. That is when he "became" learning-disabled. The teacher refers to Lou as "really learning-disabled," as if some of the students are not "really" learning-disabled. One boy, it is felt, isn't really handicapped, but his father, who is influential in the community, wants him to get the special attention that the program offers. Another boy is described as "really" EMH (educable mentally handicapped) but in an LD class because his parents requested it. Jason, a quick-talking, inner-city youngster, is known for his use of drugs and getting into trouble. The teacher recruited him for the class because she "wanted to do something for him." Each of the students in the class has serious academic problems.

The family backgrounds and experience of the students vary widely. Some live near the high school and come from professional families. Others come from inner-city poor or working-class families. More than half of the students are transferred in from other quadrants of the city. They come especially for the program. These students are less likely to have friends outside of the program and appear least socially integrated. There were twelve students in the class during our observations. Of these, six were black and six white. All of the black students were male, three of the white students were female. While students tended to form friendships within the same sex and race, there were friendly conversations, joking, and indications of concern across racial and gender lines. Philip helps Sara out of the room with her wheelchair. Mark, Pam, Maxine, and Philip often joke and play around. Jason and Leroy are not hostile toward the other students in the class but they remain detached. They identify with each other, and their friendship seems to be predicated on the fact that they are street-wise and have been in trouble with the police;

they do not take school too seriously. Lou and Bob appear to be the only social isolates.

Only by interviewing each student could we fully appreciate what the resource program meant to the students and, thereby, derive a sense of what integrated, functional, and community-based programming really means for these students. Sara, for example, lives near Hutton, is white, and has cerebral palsy. She is the only physically disabled student in the class. For her, the resource room is a supportive program that makes it possible for her to attend a regular neighborhood school for the first time in her school career:

I like this program. I'm happy to be in this high school. I'm proud to be with my own neighbors. I'm eighteen and last year I was in a junior high. Kids in the neighborhood would ask why I was going there and I told them they didn't have a program here. I felt real separate, real different. In junior high I only had one or two friends. I was only out of the resource class one or two classes, English and Math. Here, it is just like normal. All my classes are with everyone else. I'm treated like everybody else. I'm not different. They accept me for what I am, I guess.

I was petrified before I came here. I worried about if anyone would talk to me. I worried about my teachers. I worried about whether I could get along. Worried if I would be able to get around the building. At first, I was very insecure and used to run to Mrs. Katz all the time. Now I am more confident and only use her a little. I didn't know what I thought about what the other kids would do. I thought they'd ignore me or make fun. The LD thing, they can't see that except if they ask me to read. I worried the kids would find out. I worried that somebody would give me a note to read. What would I tell them. Should I tell them that I couldn't read? Then they would know. I can talk fine. I am not nervous, but if they gave me something to read, I'd be real nervous and then people would know.

Then there is my wheelchair. I didn't know how they [the nondisabled students] would take that. What surprised me most about the school was the people. They were so nice. You always had a few troubles. Once or twice a kid will be nasty. One kid told me that if I ran him over, he'd beat my white ass, but that is not usual. I feel that I am finally in my school. There are always some brats. One girl doesn't like me. She told me that I shouldn't be here; that I ought to be in my own room. But I am used to threats. They're just ignorant. They can't help it.

For Sara, the program's contribution is psychological as well as academic (reading).

Pam presents a somewhat different perspective. She is self-conscious about being identified with "special education." In the first semester, she failed social studies rather than ask the teacher for special help or draw attention to herself by asking her resource teacher to intercede. When we asked her how she felt about the program, she told us:

It's good, 'cause you need help and stuff and you get it here. Sometimes I don't feel good about being here. When I come here they ask, Why are you going in there? Are you dumb or something? These are just the kids around. These are my so-called friends but not my real friends. My real friends don't say anything. But I never talk to my friends about this program. I am afraid my friends would say something that would make me feel bad.

Although the program is an embarrassment to her, Pam feels strongly that it is important for her to be in it.

Leroy's life contrasts starkly with Pam's, although his attitudes about his schooling are in some ways quite similar to hers. He lives downtown in a run-down area. Born in Alabama, he came north with his mother, father, and twelve sisters and brothers before he started school. He is the youngest in his family. Only two of the twelve have finished high school. His father no longer lives at home, but he still lives in town and sees Leroy occasionally. Leroy is on parole for a robbery he was involved in two years ago. While we were observing, he again got in trouble with the police. Leroy has a CETA (Comprehensive Employment Training Act) job doing maintenance. He spends a half day at Hutton, then goes down to Hamilton, where he is in a modified mechanics program, and then goes to his job. His job provides money, which he spends on new clothes. Leroy talks slowly. Because of his solid build, he looks larger than his five-feet ten-inch height. On the day we interviewed him, he wore a black shiny shirt and black pegged pants. He wears his hair short, and although not defiant, he is often a reluctant participant in class activities. About the program, Leroy told us:

It is too late for me now. I'm gonna try to learn those basic things that might help me. I'm seventeen now. They say I missed too much time. I don't like not graduating, but they say that if I settle down, I could learn some basics and train for a job.

I've been in this program for two years and in special education all through elementary school. Being in this class gives you some problems with other people. If they know that you are in here, they don't react to you the same way. It is like they think that you are not like them. They would think that you are not smart. Like they were going to college and you're not. You are different. I would want to go to college, I would want it that way, but that ain't the way it is.

I tell some close friends that I am in this class but I wouldn't tell the others. It gives you problems. Special education means you can't keep up.

This is not a school I would want to stay at except for the program. If it wasn't for the program, I would have dropped out. I feel comfortable, but on certain days I don't feel like being around anyone. I feel frustrated. I hope those days go faster. I keep getting the work wrong and I'll ask Mrs. Katz. If I still can't get it, I get frustrated.

I want to be what I can get. All I can get is work with my hands. That's the farthest I can get in life. I don't like it, but that's what I'm told so that's what I have to think about.

Jason, like Pam and Leroy, feels embarrassed to be in a resource program, yet he thinks it is worthwhile:

I'm not like most of them. I am slow in some things but I'm not as slow as them. In some things I'm slower than your average, but in some things I'm a lot faster. I don't like being around them too much, because they give me a bad reputation. These kids, they're okay, I mean they are all right to talk to and things like that, but they are slow. Now don't get me wrong. This program helps me a lot because of Mrs. Katz. She helps me with my book reports, and when I get homework I can come and she can help me. In that way, it's really good, but I'm not as slow as them.

Jason often makes sounds of disgust during the fourth period, to show that the work is too easy for him, yet he has difficulty doing any written work. We asked Jason what he planned to do after school:

I'm gonna get me a job in a factory. I'm gonna do that and work there for about five years and make enough money and then open myself a store, a corner store, you know, selling groceries and that kind of stuff, a little beer. Can start it off small but then I will grow and then maybe I'll have me four or five different stores and big stores. You don't need a diploma to do that, to run a store or anything, but I'm gonna get me a diploma. If I could pass in college, I'd go there too. I'd love to go to college. I'd go for business.

We asked him why he was selected for the program.

Learning-disabled, that's what they labeled me. But I'm much more advanced than that. I'm not like most of the kids in this class. You see, but it will help me graduate. The only problem is that they label you that and that is the way you are going to be known for the rest of your life. When they look you up in the school records, there it is. You are that way for life. It wouldn't help you get a job, people seeing that. They don't want people with learning disabilities. All I want to do is graduate, though, that's what I need. Now, if after being labeled and I don't graduate, then you really got it bad.

This is a good program. I would say that I stand a 50 to 75 percent [better] chance of graduating than if I was in the regular class.

Mac is a sixteen-year-old black student with a friendly disposition. He carries himself with a maturity that is greater than his age. He is short and broad-shouldered. This is his first year in high school. We asked Mac about the program, whether he liked it. He said:

Mrs. Katz is trying to fix me up so I can get some music lessons. I play the bass, practice at home with a group. I'd like to get in the school band, but nothing has been happening so far. Maybe next year. I'd like to read music, but they don't know. There are lots of people playing jazz and they don't know how to read jazz. I'd like to finish here and like to go to Eastman up in Rochester. That is a good school. For me, with my special problems, it would be hard to get in.

Everybody in the class is kind of different. I really like the class, actually. The kids are nice. I'd rather be in here and have somebody to help me. If they could fix me up with some classes in music, that would be better.

I want to be known as somebody, not somebody who is on the assembly line. I want to make my own album. I want people to know me. I want to be on talk shows and be somebody.

As their comments suggest, being in Marge Katz's program means different things to each student. For most, it is a sign of their failure. On the other hand, it is a chance for success (e.g., getting a diploma, getting a job, getting into music). For some, the friends at the school make school worthwhile. For others, *not* having friends makes it worth it. All have to work at negotiating a relationship with typical students that minimizes their stigma. Some try to "pass."

Each of the students whom we interviewed had some kind of career goal that could be reinforced through functional, integrated, community-based programming. The actual curriculum of the class was geared in part to the students' needs, but it was usually more effective in terms of academic training (preparation for the minimum competency test necessary for graduation) than in functional life skills. The functional life skills program that utilized community sources was more preset or "packaged." It did not seem to reflect the very different social circumstances of the students or the particular vocational interests of each. In the basic skills (functional life skills) part of the curriculum, students learn such things as reading and ordering from a menu, restaurant language, computing sales tax, reading signs around town, reading bus schedules, locating places on maps, opening and using bank accounts, planning a budget, and understanding taxes. The teacher uses a workbook for basic skills and goes over the book and questions paragraph by paragraph with the students. Below is a description of such a lesson taken from an observer's notes:

Marge began, "What we are going to do today is apartments. Remember how to look for apartments in the paper. We started it yesterday. Now open the book to ad #1." Almost everyone had the booklet folded to that place. Marge and Alfred went around checking each one. "Look at ad # 1. Does the apartment have a stove and a refrigerator?" Somebody said, "No." A few people said, "Yes." Marge said, "Who said no? It says right there that it has a stove and refrigerator. See, it's abbreviated. Remember the list of abbreviations at the start of the lesson. What about pets?" Everyone said in unison, "No pets." Marge continued, "Remember don't guess. Look them up. What does Stu stand for?" Maxine said, "Stereo." Marge said, "Large sunny stereo? No, that's not it. Studio. What's a studio apartment?" "It's a small apartment with a small bedroom." "What's STV/Frig.?" They went to the list of abbreviations and someone said after a wait, "Stove." She said, "That's right, stove and refrigerator."

Marge went through all the abbreviations in the second ad and then the third. One had "HDW/FLRS," which stood for hardwood floors. She asked, "Anyone know what hardwood floors are? Are these hardwood floors?" Leroy said, "No these ain't hardwood. They tiles and concrete." Another abbreviation was "GDN," which stood for garden apartment. When she asked about that abbreviation, someone yelled out "garden," and Mark said, "I should have thought of that." Marge gave an explanation of a garden apartment. "It's an apartment that is low to the ground where you can look out and see the lawn or the garden." She went through more of the ads in the book.

As the content of this particular lesson reveals, examples from the book are far from the lives of the inner-city students who are in the class.

Five of the students live in city housing projects or other parts of inner-city housing and do not know about studio apartments and hardwood floors. Further, many of the prices listed in the book are unrealistic, given the current economic conditions. Yet the materials do raise some important issues for the students, for example, security deposits and slum landlords. The teacher sometimes talks about such issues, although her perspective is clearly that of a middle-class white person. Yet, she engages all students in a give and take, which seems to minimize the vast differences in the cultural experience between her and some of the students. Strangely enough, this cultural gap does not seem to influence the students' liking her. This is in part because she is very direct with them and they are direct with her. She has a quick wit and can out-talk the students. They respect her for this. In addition, her hard work and advocacy for them makes them feel she is on their side.

The second activity that dominates the resource program is the minimum competency test. In order for students to receive a high school diploma they must pass a statewide minimum competency test, in addition to accumulating the necessary course work. The teacher sees these requirements as oppressive, keeping her from providing educational experiences that the students need. But she feels that in order for her students to have a chance in life, they have to have a diploma, and she is therefore dedicated to maximizing each student's chance of getting one. She feels that what is needed to pass courses and the test is not what benefits her students the most. As she puts it:

Lou, he really needs living skills, he doesn't need Shakespeare. The same with Philip. *The Great Gatsby* and *The Glass Menagerie*, he needs like a hole in the head. He is in regular English and doing fine. I record the stories so he can listen, but he doesn't need that. Lou can't even take care of himself, so he needs the French Revolution?

What we need is a competency-based program designed for each student in the program. It is silly to have kids spend four years sitting here when it makes no sense in terms of them. Some don't get diplomas anyway.

Nevertheless, for the purpose of helping the students graduate, this teacher drilled the students for the test. She read paragraphs from a sample test, and the students had to select correct answers from a list to fill in the blanks.

As this teacher herself admits, the program could have been more relevant. The student would benefit from a more individualized program design. Our interviews with them confirmed that. Indeed, it was clear that by interviewing the students and by getting to know them, we could, as the teacher had done, discern interests that motivated the students, ones around which to build a program. Sara's desire for social integration and to read, Leroy's hope to graduate, Mac's dream of a career in music. The program was as good as it was—though certainly it could have been improved enormously through more integrated, functional and community-based programming—because the teacher did get to know, understand, and empathize with the students.

Of course, there is no easy response to Leroy, who appears to have lost hope, or for any of the students who feel the dilemma of wanting special services but not the stigma associated with them. Yet, if we take these students seriously, we will be compelled all the more to conceive how to make special services more normal, more ordinary, or how to make a supportive home base (a supportive caring teacher) part of every student's experience, or how to create curricula that touch all students personally. If we take these students seriously, then perhaps we learn that they, and all students, need opportunities to speak about themselves, of their aspirations, and of how they think they need assistance in reaching their goals.

THE PRINCIPLE OF COMMUNITY-REFERENCED INSTRUCTION

We discuss this principle last because it draws heavily on the first two. All students, both during and after the school years, participate in nonschool environments. The principle of community-referenced instruction takes seriously the educational goal of preparing students to function effectively in such environments. It requires that educators develop curriculum content and instructional methods that use the community outside the school to inform learning. It presumes that integration in school leads to integration in community life.

For traditional academic programs, community-referenced learning can occur imaginatively, historically through a variety of cultural means. The broad study of intellectual and scientific traditions and practices, whether through English, history, biology, chemistry, physics, or other courses, puts students in touch with realities far beyond the confines of school settings. Such traditional curricula approaches use the "human community" as an overall point of reference. Curricula for even young students include activities and information designed to expand their understanding and participation in their smaller neighborhood community.

So, too, the larger community beyond the school should enter and make a difference in the lives and curricula of students with handicaps. For students with disabilities the idea of community-referenced instruction extends the two principles of functionality and integration in both time and space. As with students who participate in the traditional academic world, whether in college or in a trade, so, too, students with disabilities will—one way or another—participate in the community outside and after-school settings. The question that teachers and others in school systems have raised about students with handicaps is whether or not they will be adequately prepared to function in the outside communities. Do school settings in fact prepare students with disabilities to act and interact in the total community? And if these students will be living in this community, does their education and learning focus upon preparation which is directly relevant to such a community?

Instruction that uses the community as the point of reference for content extends the principles of integration and functionality in two ways. First, it prepares students to interact with typical, nondisabled individuals, not just in school, but in all the places that define the social context of our lives. For example, settings connected to vocational activities, domestic living, and all the seemingly routine social and recreational settings and events, all compose key elements of the "community." Second, it teaches such skills of interaction and participation in situations and settings that are "natural" or typical to the activity or skill. For example, domestic skills like cooking, housekeeping, and shopping are taught in actual homes and grocery stores, vocational skills on actual job sites. In this way students learn and practice skills with the people and materials they will naturally encounter. Several of the teachers we met became "community trainers," offering the same systematic instruction in actual community settings they had previously been able to simulate only in classrooms.

"I'm really excited about it!" This teacher had been certified as a teacher of mentally retarded students and taught special education classes for six years (both elementary level and junior high) before getting a job in another school district as a "community trainer."

"Really, I do most of the same things that I have always done as a teacher; but the difference is that now the education happens out of school and in the community itself."

She paused and showed us an elaborate chart for riding city buses. Part of the training and education for each student required mobility training—skills development in getting around the community.

"I coordinate two classes at the junior high school. These are children with severe disabilities, ages thirteen to fifteen, and all of them spend at least 50 percent of their time at various community training sites on a daily basis."

The teacher—now a "community trainer"—explained how each work training program becomes part of the student's individualized education program. It is the community trainer who finds the community work sites in the first place; furthermore, student placement at this particular school was developed as a work-study option. The sites did not provide supervision, training, or money; the school people, under the direction of the community trainer, did all of that.

At a large, shiny cafeteria in a large suburban shopping mall, two students had a work placement. As we entered, the community trainer commented, "It's the interactions that make or break a placement."

One of the students was assigned the task of sorting silverware and folding napkins. It was mid-morning, about an hour before the cafeteria would open. This student was about eighteen years old and in a wheelchair. According to comments made later by a staff member, the student had—in the past—become easily frustrated and had "tantrums" of sorts. An assistant (who was a practicum student at a local university) worked with the disabled student, assisting in sorting and folding.

As we were about to leave, the practicum student pulled us aside and said that the site itself provided an important model.

"You don't see people having tantrums here," she said.

The other student with disabilities at the site could walk and communicate, but tended to be shy, easily distracted and upset. According to the community trainer, one of the biggest problems for him was to work with other people.

Yet, as he arrived for work that particular morning, this student responded "Hi" to one of the waitresses.

"You can tell, watching him . . . he's proud of being able to fill the water glasses without spilling; it makes him feel better." (One of his teachers made the comment as we observed from across the long dining room.)

A waitress looked up from cleaning tables and agreed. "You can almost talk with him now. Before . . . he would hardly ever look at you."

And what were they learning that couldn't be taught in the classroom, we asked? We had withdrawn from the two students and sat at one of the corner tables at the back of a large dining area. One of the students' teachers sipped coffee with us and thought about this different sort of education. For her, there seemed to be three major benefits of the community-based vocational approach.

The first appeared to be that training in actual workplaces solved the problems connected to simulations—the problem of transference. The teacher indicated that recent research would support the contention, too; but for her, it was a practical matter.

"These kids need real skills to make out better in the real world. It's just good educational practice: teach something useful and teach it in a real setting."

Another major benefit was that the severely disabled students were seen differently (and may see themselves differently too) when they were with typical people.

"Look, most of these waitresses have never even *seen* such a severely handicapped person anywhere (except maybe in an institution). The manager himself was extremely hesitant about having our students here." She paused. "Now? He loves it! These two students are punctual; they do the work without complaining; we provide the supervision; and the manager says that set-up time for the waitresses has been eased somewhat."

"Frankly, the third major benefit may be the key," commented the teacher. "Getting these kids out of the classrooms has made such a difference for us—the teachers. You couldn't imagine it."

The community trainer agreed and said that we could actually see some progress.

"The whole approach gives a lot more hope to these kids. After all, the expectations for Micky [observed in the wheelchair, folding napkins] cannot be great. Yet, this job—carefully planned and monitored—shows him (and the rest of us) that he can succeed at something."

Both teachers felt that the overall direction of community training made sense in the long term too. After all, they argued, these students with the more severe handicaps are not going to remain in school forever.

"They need some basic skills in order to survive better in the world. They need real work; they need to be able to shop (to the best of their abilities); and they need to be able to play. These things take time and training in real settings. That's what's so exciting. We're teaching skills and attitudes that will actually be useful for the rest of their lives!"

In one school district in the Midwest, for example, the district decided to rent a house in order to instruct the students with disabilities in "domestic living skills." We observed a teacher and an aide (now a domestic living trainer and an aide) with four different students at a time. For three days and two nights a week for two weeks at a time, four high-school-age students (from seventeen to nearly twenty-one years old) lived at the small, rented house and learned to cook, clean, shop, and eat together. Teachers (now domestic trainers) used systematic instructional techniques, with detailed charting of data on each student's performance. The important point to note is this: As part of their educational program at the high school, students with handicaps learned a number of domestic living skills, including aspects of shopping, cleaning, cooking, and money management—in real-life settings—and that these skills are important for the students if they are to live with some degree of independence in the community.

In another school system, located in the South, community-referenced instruction applied to vocational education. In a small electronics company, three different students with disabilities trained on the job as part of their high school curriculum in vocational training. One student, labeled "emotionally disturbed," worked at a bench next to six older women. All of the workers, including the student (a male, about nineteen years old), used a large machine to test the "trueness" and "accuracy" of electronic chips. With this handicapped student, the school district had made formal agreements with the company for supervision and training. The school's vocational trainer (again, a former classroom teacher who had received special training) arranged for all supervision and worked through the company's floor manager. The company provided one "advocate" for each student. This advocate would spend time with the student at various breaks as well as lunch. The placement would be made for ten weeks at a time. After the first few weeks, the school's vocational trainer would merely visit and confer on a weekly basis. The company's regular supervisors would provide basic oversight of the students' work.

For about fifteen students with more severe disabilities, the same school district provided job-training sites in such places as the local Holiday Inns, Howard Johnson's Motor Lodges, supermarkets, college dormitories and dining halls, the public library, as well as in two different restaurants. The director of special education as well as the high school principal felt that these vocational-training sites provided students with extra benefits connected to their future in the community.

"After all," commented the high school principal, "everyone else uses the library, the markets, and so on routinely. It's just that these more severely handicapped kids are present for the first time as *full participants.*" He told about how three students with disabilities sorted bottles at a supermarket after school. "I mean, that's what many of the rest of the kids at the high school do: so many of them work after school. I had the manager of the supermarket stop me after church and say that 'Hey, those kids are all right. They've done a good job with the bottles.' I wanted to say, 'Well, what did you expect?' but simply smiled and nodded."

The special education director agreed.

"Nothing makes as much sense for our handicapped students than to teach them real, practical, functional, and useful skills," she said. "You really need to get the kids out of the school and into the community. That's all there is to it!"

What we found was this: For students with handicaps, the curricula practices had begun to change from primarily school-based models to more community-based models.

"Sometimes it's a delicate balance," said an assistant superintendent in a large, urban district in the Northeast. He explained that many students with disabilities remain in school until they "age out" after twenty-one. But most seventeen- or eighteen-year-olds leave the high school and either go to work or go to college.

"Why not apply the same rhythms and patterns to our disabled students?" he asked. "Of course," he indicated, "most of the students with disabilities do not have the skills to go to college or to get a regular job. Although some do," he added quickly. He insisted that the school system had to do better with the handicapped students.

"We need to start the transitions from school to community much earlier. Really, that's what some of the research is beginning to show, too. With the more severely disabled students, train them to shop, cook, work, and play and do it in real-life settings. Furthermore, it's critical to start early. By the time they are fourteen or fifteen, at least half the time should be spent *outside* the school settings—and the percentage should increase dramatically as the students get older."

In a school district in the southwestern United States, teachers instruct students in how to use public transportation in order to shop and get to various job sites. One of the teachers explained the process to us.

"It takes the same sort of careful, detailed planning that you would do in a classroom except the instructional skills and planning techniques apply to, say, the transportation system." The teacher explained that they do careful task analyses about the routes, the kinds of buses available to the students (particularly the issue of buses with lifts for those students with physical disabilities), the need for assistance.

"Of course, things don't always work as the schedule or front office people say. We've had students (with an aide or teacher, of course) stranded for more than an hour at various stops. You know, the driver never showed up; the bus broke down; or sometimes the wheelchair lift wouldn't work or, once, the bus didn't even stop!" The teacher pointed out the charts and graphs that they used to plan and coordinate their program for the students.

Over lunch, one of the teacher aides said that the modest training in how to travel around the city gave some of the disabled students a whole new world. "For a couple of the older girls, both in wheelchairs, it never occurred to them that they could simply go shopping downtown, alone. Family and friends had driven them everywhere. That little bit of independence really made a difference."

In sum, the principle of community-referenced instruction both complements and completes the principles of integration and functionality with two key notions:

1. On the whole, students learn new skills faster and can use them more efficiently if they learn and practice them in the actual environments where they need to use them.
2. As students get older, an increasing proportion of their school time and learning should occur in their own nonschool environments (e.g., home, parks, restaurants, workplaces).

The following list suggests strategies for involving students' communities in their curricula.

• Get to know the demands and expectations the community places on your students. Drive through their neighborhoods. Are street crossings marked by stop lights or mostly stop signs? Are there only large grocery stores or mostly small neighborhood convenience stores? Do people use subways and buses or do the students' neighbors travel mainly by car? Do kids play in parks or parking lots?

Talk with the student's family, neighbors, and school friends. What kinds of play or recreational activities are popular among the neighborhood kids—basketball or bicycling? What kinds of outings do the family take together—shopping? camping? sports?

Try to anticipate where students will go when they leave your class. Knowing the important demands and expectations of the next school *or* nonschool environment your students will enter allows you to adapt your curriculum and instruction to better prepare them.

• Target skills that are used across environments and activities. Many important skills are used in all a student's environments as part of a variety of functional activities. Basic communication and computational skills, strategies for problem solving, and techniques for making decisions and judgments are a part of preparing pancakes for breakfast, playing a game with friends, and buying lunch at a pizza place. All of these activities and environments are potential teaching situations to be exploited. Varying settings, materials, and people to teach the same important skills speeds both the learning and generalization of new skills.

• Use naturally occurring situations. It's much easier to learn when you need to use the skills anyway—when you need to tell the cafeteria worker what you want for lunch, get dressed for gym, or apply for a part-time job. The communication, dressing, and writing and working skills acquired from such situations are more quickly and firmly learned.

• Use natural settings. Practice and simulations in classrooms may help students learn some important parts of skills, but very often the differences between the real and simulated settings are too great for students to transfer successfully such classroom learning. Using the "real" setting—the grocery store, kitchen, restaurant, employment office— can not only speed learning but offers two important advantages.

(1) Natural cues—When people at a bus stop straighten and move expectantly toward the curb, it is clear the bus is arriving. Such an effective cue is difficult to simulate. Also, few classrooms can collect the varieties of soup that dominate the aisle where the bread you want your student to find is located—or simulate the sudden temperature change that lets you know you're approaching the freezer case where ice cream is found.

(2) Natural reinforcers—Drinking a soda just purchased from a store, getting off the bus on your home block, or being complimented by the job interviewer reward effort much more powerfully than the teacher's most enthusiastic "good work."

• Enlist the help of people you find in natural settings. If you want to
create age-appropriate leisure skills for an eight-year-old, talk to a few
eight-year-olds. Similarly, people working in stores, offices, and other
potential teaching settings can provide valuable information about how
people should behave in such settings. In addition, there are many
instinctively good teachers among the nonhandicapped people in natural
settings. Their assistance in working with your students both expands
your resources and heightens awareness and positive attitudes among
the general public.

CONCLUSION

We began this chapter by suggesting that mainstreaming best not rely
for its success on super teachers. While there are certainly many outstanding teachers one can point to as having been almost singlehandedly
responsible for the success of integration programs, the cost to these
teachers is high, perhaps too high. Moreover, we have cited ample evidence, both from the effective schools literature and from our own studies,
to declare that quality programs predictably emerge from particular conditions. Factors that tend to facilitate quality schooling and, therefore,
quality integrated schooling include such things as: sequentially organized
curricula, shared educational goals, clear expectations for student behavior, attention to community building, modeling by teachers of cooperative
caring behavior, active dialogue between students and teachers, high
standards and attention to homework and other assignments, support for
teachers from administrators and parents, rewards for students who demonstrate a commitment to learning, small or at least modest school size
rather than massive congregation of students, classrooms in which multiple activities can be orchestrated simultaneously, a greater proportion
of class time spent on direct instruction, and intolerance of prejudice,
stereotyping, and discrimination.

Further, we found that three basic principles provide the foundation
for successful integration. These are (a) a commitment to integration as
a value, (b) utilization of functional curricula and a functional model (as
contrasted with a developmental approach or a strictly clinical model),
and (c) community-referenced instruction. In the discussion on integration as a value we noted the important, if obvious, finding that integration
requires active, structured intervention. In one extended example, we

described a classroom in which the teacher, Mrs. Fosse, intervened little. When she did intervene, she often did so in a manner that only made worse the negative interactions between disabled and nondisabled students. In another extended example, we described how a teacher, Mrs. Lake, successfully intervened in what initially seemed to be an integrated classroom in which a disabled student was isolated. From these and scores of other situations we have culled principles for intervention. These include such strategies as structuring integration through particular activities, integrating support services so that disabled students do not have to leave the classroom so often, teaching about differences, teachers modeling interaction with disabled students, and enlisting nondisabled students to help disabled students.

Functional programming is an approach that presumes the students will participate—however differently—in the life of society. Although there may be many levels of participation (for some students, advanced calculus may be essential; for others, partial participation in grocery shopping may be equally essential), all students should be challenged and trained to participate in society. The idea of "functional" means that students will perform actions and tasks which are characteristic of, and appropriate for, their particular abilities. Thus, a functional approach has a relative, comparative meaning depending upon the abilities and interests of particular students. Integrated school programs provide the first structured setting in which to begin a functional curriculum. For example, severely disabled students can use the typical school as a proving ground for learning appropriate social behaviors that they will need to succeed in community living.

The third principle, community-referenced instruction, suggests that students need to learn things which are geared to the opportunities available in their communities. Here we have noted the utility of such concepts as natural settings, natural cues, natural situations, skills targeted across environments, and partial as well as full participation.

Through these and other principles discussed in this chapter, it is clear that teachers can play a critical role in making integration work if they have both a supportive context (i.e., willing allies in the form of administrators, other teachers, and parents) and the practical strategies and principles with which to work. Under the right conditions, teaching, the front line, need not be so dangerous or lonely as it so often seems.

4

School District Administrators: Leadership Strategies

DOUGLAS BIKLEN AND STEVEN J. TAYLOR

Who owns special education? In some districts, it belongs to special education directors. In other districts, the director of pupil personnel or the director of instructional programs controls special education. Many administrators say that no matter who holds the program directorship, the budget officer really makes all critical decisions. In some school districts, the school psychology staff have the upper hand. And in a few districts, superintendents make program decisions.

Usually, special education belongs to many people, depending on the issue at hand and the dynamics of who cares about the issue and how it affects or is affected by such organizational factors as economics, resources, staffing, and use of space.

In the vast majority of our observations, we found that special education directors were most likely to initiate and influence integration of students with disabilities into regular public schools. The initial impetus often came from parents or from regular administrators (a principal, a superintendent, a school board member), or a school board, but the special education director actually implemented the policy. Hence, we have written this chapter primarily for special education directors. However, we hasten to add that any district level administrator could adopt most of the principles and strategies disclosed in this chapter.

What does the administrator need to know in order to act, to succeed? There are at least three major, critical elements. First, administrators need to know *who* makes change. Who are the decision makers? And, *how* do they make decisions, particularly special education/integration decisions? Second, administrators need to examine the principal barriers to change. And third, certainly most important, administrators need a basis for leadership. How can an administrator seize the initiative, elicit support, and institute change?

DECISION MAKERS

Who initiates and maintains integrated special education programs? The answer is not always administrators. In one urban district which serves 28,000 students, parents of young children demanded integration—many of their youngsters had attended integrated preschool and day-care programs—and finally won it over a period of years as the school district acquiesced to their demand by following a policy of "options." The options policy meant that parents had a choice between integrated or segregated schooling. Yet, in a major urban school district serving more than 80,000 students, it was the special education director who promoted integration, even against strong, vocal parent opposition. In a large rural state, the director of special education for the state, in concert with the state university, initiated integration programs statewide. In still another state, parents brought litigation to demand integration. That suit led to a consent agreement in the state's largest city. The agreement specified integration of programs, even for the most severely disabled students, as the service approach of preference. In a large urban, suburban, and rural county, we observed a deaf education program that was planned and implemented by an intermediate school district and that was located in regular public schools. This program began after parents protested against the policy of sending area deaf students to special boarding schools. It began less out of any rejection of segregation but out of desire to have the deaf students close to home. In several other settings, integration came about accidentally and incrementally. In one case, for example, an administrator agreed to take in a child with severe behavioral problems. Within a few years the school became known as a model integration site.

In our observations we found that the decision to integrate special education programs in regular schools occurs in one or some combination of three roles or groups: a strong administrator, a specialist, and parents.

Strong Administrator

A principal, superintendent, special education director, or other administrator makes integration an important goal. In one large southwestern urban school district, for example, administrators decided to close a segregated school—indeed, they sold it to a private vocational technical institute—and to integrate the students with disabilities into a half-dozen of the regular public schools. The decision to integrate was promoted and defended by the top level administrators. In another district, noted in chapter two, a principal welcomed the opportunity to integrate severely disabled students in a regular high school because he saw it as a strategy of enhancing the reputation of his school.

Specialist Model

A few integrated programs have begun when an individual specialist, either a teacher, a university faculty member, or a psychology staff member, can convince other leaders in the school district that the integrated approach makes good sense clinically. In one large suburban/rural multidistrict area, a university special education faculty member provided curricula and program designs, all of which were based on integrating disabled and nondisabled students. The administrators accepted the model and began to implement it.

Parents

Some schools and districts integrate disabled and nondisabled students because they regard it as their legal obligation under the "least restrictive environment" provision of federal education laws or because the courts have ordered them to integrate. In each of these cases, parents have initiated legal action. Parents have also lobbied school boards and administrators for integration. In more than a half of the integration programs we observed, parents had been instrumental in their development. Often parents enlisted support from the public (e.g., civic groups, church groups).

The Good Administrator

Ideally, the pro-integration administrator can mobilize leadership not only among other administrators but also among specialists and parents.

Administrators who want to influence the shape and location of special education services in a school district need to know how decisions are made. They must know the key actors, their interests and ideas. They need to know where and how to find support for their goals. And they need to know who opposes special education—believe it or not there are people, sometimes influential people, in every district who regard special education as little more than a problem, something to be "contained." We found numerous instances where superintendents and other high level school administrators spoke about special education as a "burden (economic) on the district." Yet, a quick analysis of cost information showed that special education programs were often actually "money makers." That is, special education programs were generating more money in what is called excess funding or state reimbursement than the programs were actually costing the school district to operate. So the real problem in such situations was attitudinal. It is important to discover the pockets of opposition as well as support.

Because no school district or group of administrators precisely resembles another, no one can predict how particular decisions will be made. But successful administrators have a good feel for such matters in their own districts. Most derive their understanding by listening and by analyzing what they learn. In the following brief exercise, we suggest a way for administrators to understand the dynamics of decision making in their own districts:

1. List the major special education decisions that district administrators (e.g., pupil personnel directors, special education directors, psychology staff, budget officers, director for curricula, transportation director) make. Typically, these include such matters as: program development, individual child placements, program location, staffing and resource levels for programs, placement procedures, transportation services, availability of related services, purchase of insurance for specialized programs, methods of reporting program achievements.
2. List the people who have some involvement in each type of decision.
3. List the people who will be affected most by particular decisions. For example, teachers, students, and parents might feel profoundly affected by decisions related to student/teacher ratios. These may become allies or opponents.
4. Now, for each type of decision (e.g., methods of transporting students with disabilities), list the decision makers in order of ability to influence the outcome.
5. Now, for each of the influential decision makers, indicate in a word or two next to the name of each, the main source of the person's

influence (e.g., position in the formal chain of command, a perceived professional expertise, political connections, control of "the purse strings," dogged hard work, alliances with special interest groups [such as professional associations, unions, or parent groups], access to relevant information, personal charisma, and ability to communicate effectively). With this information in hand, administrators gain three things. First, they minimize the likelihood they will be surprised by any one person's or group's reaction to a change proposal. Second, they know who their potential allies and antagonists will be and, to some extent, the basis for their actions. And third, since they have discovered each person's motivation, they are more likely to know how to appeal to each person or group for support.

Every administrator whom we observed as influential on integration-related issues had a keen sense of who makes which decisions. Some referred to this sense as "keeping your ear to the ground." Others called it being "politically savvy," or "streetwise." Almost all agreed, "You have to know what's going on." Making a decision, even one like integrating students with disabilities into regular schools, was never *just* a substantive or programmatic decision of doing what is right. Integration decisions always occur in some historical context. Hence the need to understand how and for what reasons decisions get made. In one district, for example, some parents and the special education director wanted to integrate special education for moderately retarded students into regular public schools. But, just two years earlier the district had built a small school (150-student capacity) for disabled students only. The parents of older disabled students (ages fifteen to twenty-one) naturally resisted any talk of integration. They had fought long and hard to win the new school building. They were not about to give it up. They feared that losing the building would mean losing the district's commitment to educating their sons and daughters. Previously, the district had housed special education in a separate, dilapidated and condemned school building and then in a modern church. The District School Board was committed to the separate school it had just built. Thus, the special education director faced almost certain, vocal opposition to his integration proposals. Consequently, he developed a strategy that reflected the reality of potential opposition. He pursued a strategy of integration by placing all programs for disabled students entering the district for the first time into regular public schools; developing a policy of options (cited earlier) whereby parents who wanted integration could have it; making it known that he believed the legal requirement to serve students in the least restrictive setting made it impossible to defend segregated programming; finding alternative uses for free space that became available in the separate school as a result of the options policy (he installed an early childhood program that he knew would not be objectionable to parents who favored segregation); introducing inservice teacher-training activities that demonstrated the benefits and potential of integration; and expanding the numbers of integrated programs annually. Moreover, after several years, students and families that had known only segregation were graduating.

Special education directors often speak of finances as the biggest disincentive to integrating. Many suburban and rural districts secure special education programs through cooperative, collaborative, or intermediate school districts. These large, special purpose school districts can operate programs in space they rent from local districts, but often they lease or build their own facilities. Local special education directors often find it difficult to create their own integrated programs unless they can convince their superintendents and school boards that a local integrated program would be operated at the same or less cost than the multidistrict segregated program. The point is that administrators who favor and want to initiate integration must contend with the others (e.g., school boards, parents who have a particular history with an existing program) who may have a special stake in the decision.

A superintendent of an urban school district wanted to create a new special education program in a junior high school for severely and profoundly retarded students who had previously not been served in public school at all. The superintendent found the special education director "too passive." The superintendent decided to move ahead on his own. He did not have any particular knowledge of the field other than that a close relative was retarded. He recognized that the program would require competent staff and, more importantly, that if the program were to succeed and pave the way for similar programs elsewhere in the district, this first such program would need a supportive school administration. The superintendent selected a school where the principal was regarded as an effective leader, one who had control in the building, and someone who would be open to a new program. This was just one more case in which a top level administrator knew what he wanted to accomplish but at the same time recognized that it was possible to select either favorable or unfavorable (e.g., hostile administrator) conditions under which to implement it. The following are additional administrative strategies that we observed in the course of our observations:

- *Trial balloons*. Ask selected administrators how they think others might react to an idea. Some administrators locate informal advisers outside of the school district administrative hierarchy from whom to seek advice.
- *Conflict Analysis*. Make a list of the most noteworthy decision conflicts in the district over the past several years. Which administrators took which positions? What seemed to motivate them?
- *Learning from History*. How have schools coped with racial desegregation? How have schools adapted to new curricula, for example the "new math" or "reading in the content areas"? Since many of the concerns related to special education integration are organizational issues (e.g., resources, attitudes, power), even completely unrelated change efforts will undoubtedly reveal much about this issue.
- *Preferred Issues*. With what kind of issues do administrators like to be associated? What ones make them nervous? Which issues that raise diverse and seemingly unmanageable animosity worry administrators? We refer to such issues (e.g., school closings, declining tax base, excessive administrative staff) as "no-win situations." Administrators want to be associated with issues and decisions that generate enthusiasm. We must find ways of making the integration issue popular. For example, one special education director has lobbied with the school board, superintendent, and administrative staff for integrated special education programs by showing that bringing these programs back (from self-contained county-run schools and private schools) can minimize school closings or help buttress arguments in favor of school construction.
- *Rewards Search*. Good administrators know how to motivate staff. Most people agree that the best way to do this is by example, by building people's confidence, by sharing explicit expectations and means of evaluating performance, and by a clear reward system. But to discover a meaningful reward for someone, we must ask the question "What motivates particular administrators, teachers, and parents?" This usually takes a good deal of time to develop, for it involves: learning why people take the positions they do on a range of issues; asking how different people spend their time; asking them what they consider their most important accomplishments; and, conversely, asking them what they find most troublesome (i.e., least rewarding) in their work and, more broadly, in the schools.

BARRIERS TO INTEGRATION

In the third section of this chapter we outline and explain specific steps that administrators can take to promote integration. But before we embark on a discussion of strategies or what might be called "the answer," we think it behooves us to examine the problem further. What is the problem? Why has integration been such a challenge to public schools? Why has the concept of least restrictive environment been so controversial?

Certain specifiable/predictable barriers stand in the way of providing an appropriate public education to all students with disabilities even to those students currently served in regular public schools. These barriers are: technological; attitudinal; jurisdictional; administrative; political; architectural; economic; personnel; logistical; legal; motivational; and idiosyncratic. Many of these barriers overlap or interact with one another. Other barriers certainly exist as well, though any others could probably be subsumed under one of these. Further, more than one barrier may stand in the way of any specific group of disabled students receiving an individualized education.

Technological Barriers

In order to meet individual education needs of students with disabilities, educational technologies must be developed, made accessible, and used. Educational technologies utilize a variety of methods for imparting knowledge and ideally use all available resources for this from the printed word to video disc to human beings. Here we want to consider the educational technology related most directly to programming issues—curriculum, instructional devices, modes of instruction, and related services. The past decade has witnessed a dramatic growth in the availability of educational technologies for the hardest-to-serve students. Yet technologies for certain groups of students, notably the severely emotionally disturbed, remain either underdeveloped or not widely accessible to practitioners. Depending on the population of students, technological barriers may involve assessment procedures (especially in the case of bilingual children), educational curriculum, or related services—for instance, physical and occupational therapy. Groups of students especially affected by technological barriers are the following: the severely disabled, behaviorally handicapped, severely and profoundly retarded, multiply handicapped, medically fragile, autistic, bilingual students, special age groups (e.g., the over twenty-one or "aging out," the very young), and older youth who need vocational training.

Promising practices for overcoming technological barriers may include the following:

- Nonbiased assessment procedures (especially for bilingual children)
- Vocational or educational curricula (for example, functional life skills training, behavioral interventions, communication skills, socialization skills)
- Specific components of an educational curriculum (for example, strategies for increasing interaction between severely handicapped and nonhandicapped students; ways of adapting devices, skill sequences, and environments for use by severely handicapped students)
- Professional (related services) interventions for severely disabled students
- Ways of training and supporting educational staff (for example, consultant teachers, inservice education)

Attitudinal Barriers

As implied by the enactment of Title VI of the Civil Rights Act of 1964 and Section 504 of the Rehabilitation Act of 1973, attitudinal barriers—specifically, societal discrimination against minority group members—have posed perhaps the most formidable obstacles to educational equity for certain groups of students. With regard to schools, attitudinal barriers may be found among school personnel at all levels (especially regular school staff), typical students, parents of typical children, school board members, and indirectly, local taxpayers. These must be countered consciously and systematically. Today, the students with difficulties most affected by attitudinal barriers are racial and cultural minorities, severely handicapped people, and students stigmatized by certain conditions (e.g., Hepatitis B carriers).

Jurisdictional Barriers

Traditionally, many disabled students have been denied their educational rights because of jurisdictional disputes between education agencies and various service systems. These disputes affect the following groups of students:

- Adjudicated youth in juvenile justice system
- Students "out-of-home"—in institutions, group homes, or foster homes
- Students on American Indian reservations
- Students on military bases
- Older youth served by vocational rehabilitation agencies
- Medically fragile students served by health-related agencies

With regard to jurisdictional barriers, promising practices are administrative and funding mechanisms designed to establish responsibility for services and to encourage coordination among different agencies. The following serve as examples of such mechanisms:

- Legal and policy mandates
- Interagency agreements
- Funding arrangements (e.g., fixed responsibility for paying the costs of services; procedures to insure that the funding "follows the student")
- Monitoring and evaluation systems
- Arrangements for transportation
- Case management services or other coordination mechanisms

Administrative Barriers

Administrative barriers are practices and policies that hinder the attainment of full educational rights for children with disabilities. Administrative barriers may include coordination and communication breakdowns between special and regular staff (between special education directors and school principals) and the current existence of separate schools serving only disabled students.

Promising practices addressing these barriers might include the following:

- Policies that clearly delineate the roles and responsibilities of regular and special education personnel
- Plans and procedures for integrating disabled children into regular schools and using special schools for alternative purposes

Political Barriers

These are barriers involving the ability of parents and/or guardians and children themselves to advocate for students' rights. Before the passage of P.L. 94–142, consumers had limited means by which to challenge school-system decisions. While P.L. 94–142 mandates parental involvement in educational decision making and provides specific due-process procedures, political barriers stand in the way of certain students' rights to an appropriate education. The following students are affected by this barrier:

- Adjudicated youth
- Institutionalized children and youth
- Children in foster care or group homes
- Children whose parents and/or guardians lack the necessary resources (e.g., information about rights, access to legal or advocacy groups) to advocate for their rights
- Children whose parents and/or guardians are not actively involved in their education and who lack surrogate parents

Promising practices designed to protect students' educational rights might include the following:

- Rights materials and training for parents and students
- Grievance procedures to resolve disputes short of formal hearings
- Methods of involving parents or guardians in educational decision making
- Provisions for recruiting and training surrogate parents

Architectural Barriers

As implied by Section 504 and its regulations, architectural barriers have excluded disabled persons from the benefits of federally assisted programs, including education. Physically and multiply disabled students, including students with mobility, visual, and hearing impairments, are obvious examples of people who may be unserved or inappropriately served because of architectural barriers. Cost-effective methods of ensuring accessibility exist (e.g., use of braille signs, cups next to water fountains, distribution of full range of school services on a single floor of building; see Barnes et al., 1978, and Hale, 1979).

Economic Barriers

While lack of funds is not a legally acceptable excuse for the violation of students' rights, disabled children are sometimes denied an appropriate education owing to economic barriers. Some disabled students live where schools are financially overburdened or where human services are generally lacking. Clearly, severely disabled and multiply handicapped students for whom educational costs are extensive are most likely to be unserved or underserved because of economic factors. However, economic barriers may hinder the attainment of equal educational opportunity for all students with handicaps. Promising practices in the area of economics might include

- The use of existing generic facilities for educational purposes
- Recruitment and use of volunteers
- Reductions in administrative or noneducational costs
- Resource sharing between agencies and departments

Personnel Barriers

For some disabled students, the unavailability of trained special educators and professionals poses a major barrier to the attainment of full educational rights. Schools sometimes have difficulty recruiting skilled and licensed professionals in the areas of physical therapy, occupational therapy, adaptive physical education, sign language instruction, and other services. Further, our interviews with state and local education agency personnel and consumers in the U.S. Virgin Islands, for example, indicate that there is a dramatic shortage of trained special educators in this U.S. territory (a complicating factor is the schools' extraordinarily high annual turnover rate owing to the fact that most special educators come from the continental U.S. and stay in the Virgin Islands for one year or less). All disabled students may suffer from a lack of trained personnel, but students with the most intensive needs—namely, those who are severely disabled—suffer most. Practices designed to overcome personnel barriers may include staff incentives to reduce turnover, cooperative staff-sharing or training arrangements with other service settings or universities, and retraining of existing staff in other areas with staff surpluses.

Logistical Barriers

Logistical barriers (e.g., the difficulty of arranging services in sparsely populated areas) may prevent disabled students from being provided with an appropriate education. Promising practices in rural areas might include: cooperative arrangements between school districts, mobile assessment teams, and regional specialists to consult with teachers on educating students with disabilities.

Legal Barriers

Before the passage of P.L. 94–142, equal educational opportunity was not mandated nationally for children with disabilities. To the contrary, education laws in many states specifically excluded certain categories of disabled children from the benefits of a public education. Many secondary level handicapped youth have not received an adequate education in the regular school environment. Thus, federal courts (see, for example, *Mills v. Board of Education*, 1972, and *PARC v. Penn,* 1971) first established the mandate for schools in some states to serve children with handicapping conditions in the years preceding congressional enactment of P.L. 94–142. Yet today legal barriers—namely, absence of a mandate nationally—prevent young children from being provided with an appropriate educational program. Although some states—such as Michigan—mandate education for all children from birth, most state education laws do not require that preschool children be provided with a public education.

Motivational Barriers

The term *motivational* is used to refer to school-aged youth who, owing to lack of motivation, negative school experiences, family circumstances, or other factors, decide to leave school prematurely. These youth are commonly referred to as "dropouts" or "push-outs." Clearly, this problem affects the typical school population as much as, if not more than, students with disabilities. Indeed, one of the largest school districts in our two studies reported that this was not a problem in special education.

Strategies for encouraging students to stay in school might include: aggressive and supportive guidance counseling, adaptations in the school curriculum, and work-study programs.

Other Barriers

Apart from systemic barriers to an appropriate public education, there are a host of idiosyncratic barriers having to do with the situations of individual students and families, which may result in their educational needs not being met.

LEADERSHIP STRATEGIES

Without district administrators' support, most principals and teachers will agree, integration is difficult. Special education directors usually have partial or complete control over student assessment and placement committees; they can influence district budget decisions; and they can provide support staff or withhold them. In this section we report on specific, practical strategies that administrators have used effectively to integrate students with disabilities into regular public schools.

In one small to moderately sized suburban/rural school district we met a special education director who typifies how administrators can promote integration. Prior to becoming special education director, she had been a resource teacher in the district. In this role, over twelve years ago, she talked the district into bringing a severely disabled child back to the regular schools from a segregated out-of-district placement. At the time, after observing the child, a school principal remarked to her, "Don't you think you have bitten off a lot more than you can chew? Why, this child is nothing but an animal. This child looks more like an animal than a person." Since then, largely because of this special education director's leadership, the district has become known for its innovative special education program. The district now serves three hundred special education students directly. At a recent school board meeting, the superintendent credited the special education director as almost solely responsible for this reputation. One teacher describes the director's role: "I think she was a model for a lot of staff. And because she was willing to take a risk, they would take a risk also."

What does it mean to take risks? What does it mean to provide teachers with support? What principles guide administrators in program development, in curriculum selection, in staffing, in planning a new program? How do administrators predict the kind of difficulties they will encounter? What does a special education director need to know in order to make a good fiscal argument in favor of integration? In this section we will address these and other questions related to the administrator's role in promoting integration.

Commentators on integration and mainstreaming all advise planning:

> There are no magic tricks in developing and implementing a sound mainstreaming program in a school. The basic principles are those of good planning and management. There are very interesting and complex dynamics involved in mainstreaming, of which the administrator and the staff need to be aware. (Paul, et al., 1977, pp. 130–31)

Indeed mainstreaming and what we have chosen to call integration are complex. Yet, in a certain sense, while we have argued that administrators must approach their school district as a unique context, with its own dynamics, we have identified particular patterns that integration takes (e.g., islands in the mainstream, teacher deals, unconditional mainstreaming, dual systems). Every existing program should fit one or a combination of these types of integration. Similarly, we dispute the notion that each school district must discover the basic principles by which to promote integration. Paul and his colleagues have implied that any principles, even contradictory ones, will do:

> The principal and staff need a mainstreaming model or approach and they need to share in developing it. Whether it is a cascade of services, a resource room approach, contracting, total integration, advocacy, or some other general approach or combination of approaches, they need to know the way mainstreaming is to be approached in their building. (Paul, et al., 1977, p. 131)

We agree, of course, that principals and staff need a shared vision, a guiding approach. We agree too that they should participate in formulating the approach. Yet we disagree with the suggestion that almost any approach will suffice. In fact, we have observed in dozens of classrooms and schools that there are a variety of basic principles emerging in the field which go beyond commonly accepted administrative practices of good management (e.g., monitoring, accountability, chain-of-command decision making, articulation of goals and objectives, evaluative measures, and strategies of reinforcement) and which, in far more specific terms, can guide integration. While principals and staff can and should collaborate in giving these principles meaning within their own schools and classrooms, district level administrators can provide leadership by articulating the broad guiding principles by which all implementation, all problems, and all planning can be measured.

The following are principles and practices that administrators and program staff across the country have increasingly adopted as effective for facilitating integration:

Normal Patterns

The pattern or schedule of a student's day, no matter how filled with specialized services and curricula, should resemble the flow of events for a nondisabled student. Students with disabilities should come to school at the same time as other students, should participate in school assemblies, should have opportunities for after-school extracurricular activities when other nondisabled students do, and should attend typical homerooms. As we have stated previously, "Try to create as normal as possible an experience for disabled . . . [students] in the school. If, for example, nondisabled . . . [students] have lockers, then so should disabled . . . [students]. If nondisabled . . . [students] have homework, then so (too) should disabled . . . [students]" (Biklen and Sokoloff, 1978, p. 20).

Continuity in Location

To the extent that educators regard special education as an "add on" service, it is expendable. That is, when a school becomes overcrowded, the special education program is the one likely to be moved. Administrators can make a commitment to locate certain types of programs (e.g., a class for multiply disabled students, a class for students with severe autism, a deaf education program) in particular elementary, junior/middle, and high schools over five- and ten-year periods so as to ensure that students entering programs at the lowest grade or age level can be as assured as nondisabled students that they will be able to attend this same school as long as they are of age. The practice of shifting special education programs from building to building, even from one district to another, year after year, destroys any chance that students with disabilities will be able to develop lasting friendships with their nondisabled peers and faculty.

Ordinary Language

Special educators have a penchant for special language, for jargon. We use such terms as *clinical instruction* instead of *teaching*. We speak of *treatment* rather than *service* or *education*. And we develop many more technical terms to describe events and activities that probably could be described as well in ordinary language. Each time we use more specialized terms or acronyms, particularly when we fail to explain them to the uninitiated (non–special education staff, parents, citizens), we exclude people from equal participation in a conversation and in decision making related to special education. We recommend a policy, demonstrated by the special education director's own practice, of minimizing specialist language when ordinary language would suffice.

Functional Programs

What is the goal of special education? Is it to fill time? Is it to teach skills? If it is the latter, then for what purpose do we teach skills? What expectations do schools hold for disabled students after they leave school? The majority of severely disabled students have always gone into sheltered workshops and day-treatment or day-activity programs after leaving the public schools. If these programs were unavailable, they often stayed at home and did nothing in particular. Of course, some students, with the help of their families, found work and recreation activities in more integrated settings. In recent years, several school districts have aggressively sought to help students make the transition from school to community life. One urban district in which we observed now places all of its severely disabled students in community work settings after they leave school. That practice has been facilitated largely by the introduction of functional training. For a discussion and explanation of functional programming see the previous chapter on teachers.

Charting Progress

It is common that educators require students to demonstrate what they have learned. It is less common for school systems to require the same accountability for themselves. Yet, in many of the more lively programs we observed, administrators and teachers alike could point to countless concrete examples of progress. These examples include child change data (a child who had no expressive language is now saying a few words; a student who has never held a job before is working in a job for which the school trained him; a student who had been disruptive in class has developed excellent classroom behavior), evidence of expanded opportunities for students to learn (e.g., introduction of a new vocational curriculum), parents' assessments of new programs and their effects on their youngsters and their own lives, evidence of support for the programs from non–special education staff in the schools, and evidence that programs now serve a broader range of students and, increasingly, more and more severely disabled students. Administrators need to work with staff in identifying measures of success. These prove extremely important to the dynamics of a program. If staff feel that an administrator cares enough about a program to expect results or to collect information about it, they will tend to respond with added enthusiasm. If administrators, staff, and parents alike can chart developments such as those noted above, this evidence of progress will likely generate feelings of optimism for the future. After all, if progress has been possible in one or several areas, this bodes well for similar change efforts in other areas.

Grouping by Age

In his book, *The Principle of Normalization in Human Services*, Wolfensberger (1972) presents the concept of serving people with disabilities in "age-appropriate" settings. That is, we should not encourage or ask adults to play with dolls. We should not group high-school-age students in special programs or schools with elementary-age students. Whenever we do group students in such atypical ways, we communicate a message, albeit often unstated, that the older disabled student is really childlike and should be treated as such and should be expected to act as such. This practice of treating older disabled people as we would treat children many years younger has a long tradition. In part it was encouraged by the psychological concept of developmental growth and in part by the notion of mental age. The basic idea of developmental psychology is that children mature behaviorally in more or less predictable developmental stages. A person cannot jump to an advanced developmental level without first having passed through a lower or less advanced level. People develop in sequence. It is easy to see how special educators might have helped reinforce the stereotype of teenager-as-toddler by equating developmental performance of the severely disabled teenager with the nondisabled youngsters. Now, with the principle of normalization, we are suggesting that irrespective of a student's behavioral performance, it is possible to group students and to teach them in ways that are more in keeping with their age. For example, place high-school-age disabled students in special programs in regular high schools. Similarly, despite a student's inability to perform at age level on particular developmental tasks, it is possible to teach the same students with materials and contexts that are appropriate to their age level. Instead of sorting geometrically shaped colored blocks, a high-school-age student might learn to apply sorting skills within the context of putting silverware away. Instead of learning the concept of object permanence by watching a teacher hide a colored ball or a child's doll, a high school student might observe a teacher placing colorful magazines (e.g., *Sports Illustrated, Life*) in a cabinet. The principle of grouping by age can prove useful in evaluating virtually every new program idea whether it occurs in the classroom or at the district level (e.g., decisions on how to transport students with disabilities to school, location of school programs, selection of district-wide curriculum materials, authorization of field trips).

Integrating Widely

We have observed many school districts and one state where school officials have decided to phase out segregated schools. Many districts have either converted the use of segregated facilities, refused to contract for segregated services, or have sold the segregated facilities if they were part of the district's facilities. Hence, we find more and more students with disabilities dispersed throughout regular public schools. But, we have found no single approach to the dispersal. Some districts attempt to adhere to the "principle of natural proportions"; for example, that the proportion of severely disabled students at a regular school should approximate their proportion in the general school population, approximately 1 percent (Brown, et al., 1977; Sailor, Wilcox and Brown, 1980). If we considered the entire disabled school population, natural proportions would mean about 6 to 10 percent of each school's population should be disabled. In one district that integrated severely disabled students by natural proportions, we found anywhere from one to five classes spread throughout a dozen separate elementary, middle, and high schools. The largest number of severely handicapped students at any single school is 35 out of a total school population of 2,000 or 1.75 percent. Another large, southern urban district has 85 students with profound mental retardation who attend fifteen classes in nine separate schools. In rural states we observed many instances where schools contained single classes of severely disabled students. In still other districts we observed far larger concentrations of special educational programs and students in fewer schools. In one urban district, certain schools were labeled as preferred sites for special education programs. Half of one small elementary school's classes were for special education. Another elementary school housed the district's only autism programs as well as three other programs for severely disabled students and several resource programs for mildly disabled students. In another large urban district, the special education department disperses eight or more special education classes for severely handicapped students in each of seven regular schools. The number of students with severe disabilities ranges from 60 to 88 in six elementary and middle schools while the high school serves 134 severely handicapped students out of a population of roughly 3,000 (4.5 percent). While it is obvious that greater congregation of special programs may offer certain logistical and administrative advantages in terms of staffing, provision of related services, and monitoring, it also probably limits the degree of social integration at each school. We found, too, that schools which integrated very large numbers of disabled students (half of the student body) were widely known in the community as "special schools." In their efforts to resolve the problem of how best to disperse special education programs from segregated to integrated settings, school districts have evolved several potentially useful principles: (a) place students as close as possible to the schools they would attend if they were not handicapped; in many instances school districts have been successful in placing students in what would have been their home school anyway; (b) place students with disabilities in schools that serve their age group; (c) avoid creating large concentrations of programs in only a few schools; (d) when initiating new programs, select schools in which principals and other staff are likely to be receptive; and (e) locate special education programs in as many different schools in a single district as possible.

Equal Importance

Wherever there has been a history of not educating students with disabilities or of segregating them, the concept of integrating these students into regular schools has been regarded, at least in some quarters, as an experiment. Programs for students with disabilities have been perceived as an "add on." This is essentially the attitude that lurks behind such seemingly reasonable questions as "Where will the money come to serve these children?" or "I am not sure we can afford the extra burden of special education; how do you propose we make ends meet if we take on the special ed kids?"

Special education is not an add-on service. It is part of regular public education. We need to approach it from that perspective. District administrators need to be able to speak of special education advances in much the same way that they now speak of the public schools' creative approaches to the humanities or their commitment and progress in science and math education, which are so essential to high technology development. And indeed administrators have much they could talk about. Take, for example, the enormous growth of knowledge in the area of augmentative communication where special educators and allied professions have applied computer technology to assisting people with very severe disabilities to communicate by using computers, voice boxes, optical scanners, and similar devices. People who had never before spoken are communicating volumes. People who could not give so simple a message as, "I am bored" or "I would like to have a piece of fruit," can do so! Think of the remarkable developments in the field of autism. Just two decades ago, the concept of autism had recently been reported in the literature. Experts thought that it was a psychiatric problem, the solution to which was therapy, both for children so afflicted and for their mothers who were presumed to have precipitated the condition by their cold rejection of their child. Little thought was given to educating such children. Slowly, however, educators began to develop alternative theories to the psychiatric one. How could you explain, after all, the seemingly bizarre peaks and valleys of an autistic child's performance? Educators began to educate autistic students in experimental but effective programs (Schopler and

Olly, in press; Knoblock, 1982) with much success. Now, educational intervention has firmly proven that autistic students can develop toward far greater independence than ever imagined even though we still do not know autism's origins. Special educators need to communicate the performance and promise of special education, for such developments suggest the field's equal importance alongside other areas of education.

Delabeling

We place unrealistic expectations on diagnostic processes and information. We often assume that if we know a person's disability, we can create approriate, even optimal, programs for the person. Thus, we prescribe self-contained special education for a student who has been categorized as having trainable or, to use another term for the same thing, moderate retardation. In fact, it would be difficult to find a case of a moderately retarded person who attends a regular class or, even, a resource room program. In recent years, the assumption of the field has been that trainable students can be served best in special, self-contained classrooms. While we know, at least intellectually, that there is much more to diagnosis than the production of an overarching label (e.g., retarded, autistic, learning-disabled, deaf, blind, hearing-impaired, orthopedically handicapped, visually impaired, emotionally disturbed)—any good diagnosis will establish a student's performance levels on certain dimensions, will relate skills to norms, will suggest the viability of one curricular approach over another—we frequently use diagnostic information in stereotyped ways. In many programs we visited, staff seemed to try consciously to avoid using disability categories to describe individual students. Instead, staff spoke of students' various qualities, some rather positive (e.g., "Tom has a marvelous sense of humor"; "Mary has a lot of friends"; "Ellen is outstanding in math") and some which revealed problem areas (e.g., "Charles has not yet developed expressive language"; "Peter has some gaping affective deficits"; "Joe gets frustrated easily"; "Alice needs physical therapy each day: she's severely physically involved.") This latter approach to describing students' performance and behavioral attitudes has the advantage of imparting specific information about people without defining the person by a more global category. Also, from the standpoint of an educator, the latter descriptions offer much more clear information about the student's needs and possible relevant curricula. Usually, once districts make a conscious effort to move away from everyday use of the global labels—most states still require use of the standard disability categories for classification purposes—they do so not only in such matters as teachers' reports but also in how they identify classrooms and activities. Gym for trainable students becomes just gym; the instructor and the students may know that it is modified, but there is no functional need in the school to create a special disability-related label for a gym class that serves students with disabilities. Similarly, the name of a classroom need not be "the L.D. class," but, rather, "class 101" or "Mr./Ms. Murphy's class."

Learning from the Field

In the first chapter, entitled "Getting Started," we suggested that integration is a relatively new phenomenon. Further, we noted the fact that integration takes numerous, identifiable forms in schools. That is to say, the concept of integration, while conceptualized several decades earlier, is deriving its meaning not so much from those who first conceptualized it as from those who have implemented it in schools. Thus the findings in this book are drawn almost exclusively from the lessons of daily practice, from schools, school districts, and from people who work in them or who are concerned with what they do. And, just as we have described an understanding of integration from practice, so too can administrators discover promising practices by examining programs in their own districts. We all have a tendency to listen more to the experiences of people elsewhere than in our own communities. We often overlook quality programming and true innovation when we see it every day and grow to expect it. As administrative strategy though, we strengthen local efforts by finding and bringing prominence to excellent efforts locally. In our observations we frequently met administrators who could speak knowledgeably about certain programs and staff; they seemed to hold up their performance as examples for other staff. This is a form of standard setting. By holding up one or several programs as examples, even as models, district administrators can communicate, in concrete terms, expectations for other programs in the district.

Legal and Moral Imperatives

The intent of special education law never was to end segregated schooling for students with disabilities. A more reasonable interpretation of that law is that it guaranteed first, and foremost, the right to a "free appropriate public education," and second, certain types of services and rights designed to help ensure fulfillment of the latter. The law clearly afforded the right to equal educational opportunity, but it did not say every student should be educated in regular public schools. As we have noted elsewhere in this book, the call for services in "the least restrictive environment" (LRE) was remarkably unclear. A conservative or, should we say, cautious reading of the law suggests: "What this item [LRE] boils down to is that when a school district can show that the use of a regular educational environment accompanied by supplementary aids and services is not adequate to give the child what he or she needs, educational segregation is permissible" (Sarason and Doris, 1979, p. 369). Sarason and Doris go on to suggest that the law merely intended to reduce the prevalence of segregation "somewhat" (Sarason and Doris, 1979, p. 369). Yet, as Sarason and Doris are fully aware, Public Law 94–142 has at least some roots in the 1954 racial desegregation case. While P.L. 94–142 is vague, even a bit confusing, on the integration/segregation question, recent evidence of integrating students with severe disabilities into regular public schools raises the obvious question, "If you can integrate severely disabled students in one district into regular public schools, then why not in all districts?" Early arguments that more integration might be possible in urban areas where there are concentrations of disabled students, but certainly not in rural areas, have been completely overcome by the existence of sophisticated integration efforts in rural areas nationwide, in the West, Midwest, and Northeast. Thus, we might now make a statement remarkably similar to Sarason and Doris's but with the opposite conclusion; what this boils down to is that since many school districts—urban, suburban, and rural alike—have shown that they can serve even the most severely disabled students in regular educational environments (schools) when accompanied by supplementary aids and services, pleas by other districts to continue segregating their disabled students are no longer credible. Thus educational leaders can now speak unequivocally for integration as a consummately possible, as well as morally desirable, goal. The various specific elements of federal and state laws as well as recent court decisions (e.g., individual education planning, due-process rights, guarantees of related services, periodic evaluation, parent involvement, state planning, and identification of handicapped children) merely provide the tools by which to buttress the goal. And, perhaps of equal importance, people, particularly typical citizens, teachers, and parents, look to administrators for leadership in such matters. If

a school district is embarking on an important policy and set of practices—
for example, integrating students with disabilities into the public schools—
what better security can it have than to know that what appears as proper,
common, and moral sense, is also correct in terms of legal principles and
best educational practices.

Planning

Everyone agrees, integration requires careful planning and preparation (Stetson, et al., 1981; Paul, et al., 1977; Taylor, 1983; Bogdan,
1983; Stephens, et al., 1982). Where will the integrated programs be
located? How will transportation and related services be provided? How
much will it cost? How will support from principals, teachers, and parents
be obtained? How will negative attitudes be countered? How much staffing will be needed? What types of skills will staff have to exhibit? Are
the available buildings suitable for integration? Will some require modifications? These and other questions explain the need for planning.

As we have noted in the first chapter, one model of integration, which
we called "teacher deals," involves little if any planning at the district
level. In this model, teachers discuss integration between themselves and
develop strategies based on their own perceptions. Yet, as we have suggested, this model of integration is fraught with problems, not the least
of which is the lack of administrative support during implementation. In
this model, when a problem arises, teachers rarely have anywhere to turn
for help. Again, we see the need for planning, for ensuring that at least
certain basic steps have been taken prior to integrating regular and special
education programs in regular schools.

Common planning steps include the following:

- Form a task force to develop an integration plan. The task force typically
  includes teachers, parents, principals, other teacher specialists, and
  district administrators.
- Assess needs. Who are the students who will be involved and what is
  the need for the program?
- Set goals. Is the goal to create deaf education programming at the
  elementary and secondary levels, for example? If so, is there an immediate objective of developing primary level programs? The planning
  group needs to develop clear and specific understanding of the group's
  purpose.

- Conduct inservice education programs on the types of programs and the types of students to be served in the proposed program. Arrange visits for regular educators to segregated programs and for special education staff in segregated settings to regular schools.
- Meet with and involve administrators and staff at the proposed intergrated sites.
- If possible, develop curricular recommendations for existing segregated programs on how they might best prepare students for the integrated sites. This concept is frequently referred to as the "criterion of next environment," evaluating progress toward achieving skills needed in the next placement.
- Plan to locate programs in settings that are appropriate to the ages of the students with disabilities.
- Involve parents of nondisabled and disabled students in the planning process through open meetings, announcements of planning progress, solicitation of parents' advice, and similar strategies.
- Arrange for visits by the disabled students to the integrated sites.
- Identify program support needs: curriculum support, related services, general problem solving, and other support functions that are typically fulfilled by consulting teachers.
- Specify policies and procedures concerning administrative authority for the proposed program.
- Where necessary, assign a staff person to coordinate the integration effort; this could usually be accomplished in conjunction with other duties. Some districts appoint assistant principals or particular teachers to this task.
- Identify means by which the program will be evaluated.
- Prepare conversion plans for any facilities that may no longer be needed as a result of the integration.
- Develop an effective means of communicating information about new programs and existing programs and issues to other administrators, to teachers, to parents, and to the community at large. Specific communications strategies include: visibility in local media (e.g., newspapers, radio shows, even television talk shows and news), school district and program newsletters, memos, special mailings, open houses, presentations to community groups, advisory groups, brochures, program descriptions, parent handbooks, staff handbooks, annual progress reports, and multimedia presentations.

Money

The cost of social programs has always been an important theme in American public policy. How much will deinstitutionalization cost? How much will Medicaid cost? How much will Title IX (equality for the sexes in education) cost? How much will bilingual education cost? How much for mass transit? How much for food stamps? Like each of these questions, the question "How much will integration cost?" demands a response. To answer the question we must first know a bit about the financing of schooling in general.

Teachers, related-services staff, and administration account for most of public educational programming costs. Buildings, transportation, and materials account for a far smaller portion of the school budget. That fact should shape any cost/benefit discussion of integrated and segregated special education. In addition, it helps to know that states develop special funding formulas to reimburse local school districts for the extra expenses associated with providing special education services to children with disabilities (see Burrello and Sage, 1979). Sometimes, the formula covers all excess costs. In other situations, the state formula covers part of the costs. Local tax revenues and federal reimbursements provide the balance. In some states, the state reimbursement formula funds segregated "special schools" more handsomely than it does comparable programs in regular local schools. A state may even provide 100 percent funding for some state-operated separate schools for disabled children and youth while providing far less generous support for programs operated by individual school districts in integrated sites. In these situations, then, the local taxpayer and the program developers have an economic incentive to segregate. Yet the actual or real cost of segregated versus integrated programming might differ. Either way, the taxpayer pays, whether by local real estate tax dollars or by state and federal tax dollars.

In a southwestern state where we observed extensive integration—in fact, one major urban district serves all of its disabled students except three, and these three are served out of district in private schools at the request of their parents—the state offers no financial "reward" for placing students in segregated schools. Thus, school districts receive the same sum of state reimbursement money whether they decide to send a student to a $20,000-per-year segregated private school or place the student in a $7,000-per-year program in a regular public school building. Child counts, which are used to determine the state's reimbursement to local districts, are, in this state, based on where a child goes to school as opposed to where he or she lives. Thus the local public school can offer programs to children and youth living beyond the boundaries of the district without elaborate interagency agreements or financial loss. The policies actually constitute real incentives for local districts to serve all students in regular public schools. In a major eastern state, however, the state provides reimbursements for excess costs (the cost of serving a child with a disability minus the cost of serving a nondisabled student) at a rate that ranges from 4 percent of excess cost to 80 percent of excess cost, depending on the wealth of the district. But all local districts, irrespective of their wealth (tax base), receive 80 percent reimbursement for every disabled student placed in a private school. This funding formula rewards segregation.

Social planners have frequently justified large programs (e.g., regional or intermediate school districts for providing specialized programs) on the grounds they would produce economies of scale. But segregated education has not generally provided economies of scale (e.g., Herbel, 1977; Rice, 1975). Large separate facilities tend to be accompanied by (a) lack of access to volunteer assistance of nondisabled students; (b) excessive transportation associated with travel to one site as opposed to multiple, dispersed sites; (c) creation of administrative and support staff that duplicate those of regular public school (including superintendents, principals, guidance staff, and psychologists); (d) need to maintain separate data systems, food service programs, and so on; (e) duplication of certain equipment and facilities such as auditoriums and swimming pools—obviously, any capital construction in times of declining enrollment has no justification. Thus, one cannot make a simple case that larger is cheaper. Nor have private schools been inexpensive. The private schools tend to inflate educational costs, for many of them are residential programs; state and local government must pay both the residential and educational costs.

It may be far easier to make the economic case for integrated, often smaller educational programs. Local schools can provide a full continuum of services, thus making it possible to utilize less restrictive services (which are less costly; see Grund, 1976; Rice, 1975) more easily. In addition, local school districts can realize lower transportation costs and the economy of not having to fund a duplicate administrative hierarchy.

Moreover, evidence now suggests the possibility of districts developing interagency agreements with nonschool human-service providers for certain related services on a cost-efficient basis (Audette, 1980). Such agreements can enable a district to provide an educational program even to a child with complex and multiple needs.

In many states, funding formulas have not been developed with an eye to maximizing integration. Thus, it is essential that administrators at the local level understand just how the funding mechanisms work and that they strategize on how to use existing funding formulas to maximum advantage. In numerous districts we observed special educators who were able to create programs in local regular schools despite fiscal incentives to send students out of their districts. The special education directors found that while the reimbursement rates favored out-of-district placement, the out-of-district placements were so much more expensive in real terms than programs that could be offered in the local district that the excess cost outweighed the effect of the funding formula.

Staffing

"But we are not trained. We don't have the skills to deal with those students." These words of caution and concern are often heard from teachers and principals when faced with the prospect of integrating students with disabilities in regular public schools. It is a matter that we discuss further in our chapter on teachers. But it is also an issue that concerns district-level administrators, for it is they who must allay such fears.

In the course of our observations we encountered this concern frequently. Yet we found that the spoken concern could not always be taken at face value. As one observer reports:

In spite of the fact that lack of training seemed to be a continuing lament, only two of the teachers actively sought help from the special education staff or resource personnel. Interestingly, one of the two was the most vocal opponent initially. In fact, the teacher whose initial response was most favorable to integration ("kids are kids; I'll take them.") was the least responsive to outside offers to help. One specialist described the response of this teacher: "I went over to see her and she was really indignant—like 'What do you think you can tell me . . .?' She was really on my case."

In this example, the two teachers who actively sought and received the most help were the two who apparently made the most appropriate curricular adaptations. For example, Mrs. Casey, one of the teachers, discussed various instructional strategies (e.g., modeling, using pictures, moving a student through an activity) with special education teachers—she was mainstreaming several special education students in her class. She observed the special education class and borrowed materials. Similarly, the physical education teacher met with the district consulting teacher a dozen times during the year. He was the only teacher who had the kind of individualized goals and record keeping that were also used by the special education staff. The messages for special education administrators in all of this are: (a) regular educators do need assistance in undertaking new activities; (b) teachers' initial comments about need or desire for more skills and assistance do not necessarily correspond with real interest in, or willingness to partake of, consultation services when offered; and (c) teachers must want and actually accept consultation if district-wide policies and practices are going to find their way into the local schools and classrooms.

In one state, policy and administrative leaders address this problem of teacher interest and teacher performance (i.e., taking advice) by offering special two- and three-week training sessions for special education staff who want to prepare themselves to work with severely and profoundly disabled students. Teachers volunteer for the training. In other words, they come with their own motivation. Similarly, administrators can locate new programs in schools where they know certain staff have previously demonstrated openness to change. Some special education administrators establish task forces of teachers and parents to help design integration efforts. Then, if the proposed integration appears particularly difficult (e.g., integration of disabled students into vocational programs, integration of students from an institution into regular schools, integration of students who have not previously been in public schools), the administrators often assign special coordinators to assist with implementation in the first year or two. In a rural state, the special consultant usually serves many schools and, often, more than one district. The principal responsibilities of a consulting teacher include at least the following:

- *Teacher support.* Listening to concerns of teachers, providing moral and technical support, asking questions, sharing experiences, and general problem solving.

- *Training*. Provide individual and group training on such topics as curriculum modification, educational assessment, measurement, behavioral teaching methods, individual case planning, functional curricula, utilizing community resources, developing parent narratives, and integrated therapies.
- *Ideas*. Consulting teachers can observe teacher performance in the classroom and can provide suggestions. Specialists frequently use videotape equipment in the classroom as a means of providing suggestions to teachers.
- *Assistance in case planning*. Consulting teachers can assist parents and teachers in reviewing and developing individual educational plans. Consulting teachers can help gather baseline performance data, develop possible long- and short-term goals, identify strategies for teaching goals, and formulate evaluation methods.
- *Modeling*. Consulting teachers can demonstrate teaching approaches.
- *Data collection*. Consulting teachers can assist classroom teachers in developing data collection instruments for use with individual students. Classroom data systems can provide useful information when consultant and classroom teachers get together to discuss progress.
- *Introduction of technology*. Most classroom teachers have little time to research new technologies or, even, alternative curricula. The consulting teacher can identify technology needs such as augmentative communication equipment (e.g., computer, voice box, communication board, a new switch) and can put the teacher in touch with appropriate specialists. In some instances, consulting teachers can bring new technology (e.g., a new approach to vocational programming in community settings, a new text for teachers on serving autistic students in the mainstream) directly to a teacher.

Many school districts, particularly smaller ones, do not have the luxury of a consulting teacher on staff. In such cases the special education director can fill some of these roles. The following example of a special education director's work with a veteran teacher suggests the type of forceful yet responsive role that a consultant must play. The special education director especially liked the teacher's ability to be assertive in explaining her approach to other teachers and to parents, her confidence in teaching children, and her ease at supervising aides and student teachers. The director's perceptions of this teacher are illustrated in an anecdote about a new student in the class. This student, Danny, had previously attended another kindergarten class where, according to the director, the teacher had defined him as aggressive and disturbed. The director arranged for Danny and his mother to visit the new class. At the end of the hour, when it was time to go, Danny reached up and gave Lynn (the teacher) a big hug. To the director, Danny's hug reflected his instinct about the difference between the hostile classroom environment he had come from and the climate and personality that Lynn radiates. In the words of the director, "If you've got committed people, then you can find a way to do anything. I wait for Lynn to tell me how things should be and then I work out an administrative way to make them happen." In other words, both the teacher and the director view the teacher as a leader, as someone who can give advice and yet be open enough to be observant and listening. This case exemplifies the role that special education directors and their staff (e.g., consulting teachers) can play in providing staff support and leadership.

As programs for severely and profoundly disabled students have proliferated in regular public schools, administrators have had to face increasingly complex staffing problems. Many directors have found themselves adding specialist upon specialist, including language and speech specialists, occupational therapists, physical therapists, classroom aides, as well as resource staff. In addition to the district-level logistical problems that this creates, for example of scheduling specialists for children in different programs and in different schools, it poses problems for teachers and students as well. Teachers complain of their having to become staff managers, of getting further and further removed from direct instruction as the specialists take over, of disjointed curricula when specialists' activities do not match other academic classroom activities, and of classroom and child disruption when students shuttle in and out of the classroom to specialists. (We discuss the value of integrated therapies in the chapter on teachers.) Some administrators now emphasize less sharp differentiation of staff by specialties and more communication and collaboration between staff. One statewide system for serving autistic students has adopted what it calls a "generalist" approach to staffing. Social workers learn how to conduct psychological assessments. Psychology staff learn how to work with parents in preparing narratives of their experiences with their children. Speech therapists work with staff to integrate speech and language development throughout the children's individualized education plan. As the specialists become familiar with each other's specialties, the specialties lose their mystique and the specialists can better communicate with each other. They understand each other's perspectives better. Obviously, for specialists to work together, to participate in demystifying their own professional expertise, they must have an environment that is conducive to, even rewarding of, staff sharing. The district special education director, perhaps more than any other single person, can communicate support of this generalist approach.

Finally, district-level administrators must endeavor to integrate special education staff in much the same way as they integrate students. As long as special education staff enjoy special salary differentials (apart from standard benefits that accrue to staff on the basis of years of training or experience), different holidays, different and separate inservice training programs, and so forth, the administrators merely perpetuate the separateness of special from regular education programs. Administrators must find commonsense ways of bringing staff together on hiring committees, for training, on planning committees, for social events, in extracurricular programs for students, and in myriad other ways. Staff integration is further discussed in the chapters on principals and teachers.

Parents

Administrators talk about parents. Sometimes they speak with respect and admiration. "That parent keeps pushing. She's the best advocate we have in this district." Or, "Parents are the ones who we need to hear. They spend the most time with their kids. If anyone knows their strengths and weaknesses, they do." Sometimes the talk is less flattering. In the course of our studies, we did not count administrators' negative comments. Thus we could not compare their frequency with the positive ones. Suffice to say, we heard an array of negative remarks: "Parents. I know all about parents. They know the law better than we do." "Some of them are never satisfied." "If they knew what we know, they would have us up on charges." "They're shopping for a diagnosis" (i.e., they don't like the one we have given their child). "They expect miracles."

The administrators who spoke negatively of parents had bad experiences with parents. They felt besieged by complaints. They felt bewildered by parent pressures and distrustful of parent involvement. They wanted to manage the "parent problem" or, better yet, just have it go away. Their most common perception of parents was as adversaries. Their vision of parents was as "the opposition" whom they saw on the other side of a table in a due-process hearing, or at the microphone in a public meeting, or at a parent press conference, each time complaining that the school was not doing enough.

Tension between schools and parents is nothing new. Willard Waller wrote of the conflict in his now-classic book about schooling, *The Sociology of Teaching* (1932, reissued 1976): "Parents and teachers usually live in a condition of mutual distrust and enmity" (p. 68), he wrote. "The conflict between parents and teacher is natural and inevitable . . ." (p. 69). "The irate parent is not a mere creature of literature; he is one of the facts of the social life in which teachers are involved" (p. 74). And, finally, the teacher "has not confidence enough in the essential security of his position to allow attacks to be made upon it without at once sending out a punitive expedition" (p. 77). And so the conflict of parents and schools escalates. Of course school administrators are, in the vast majority, former teachers. Hence they come to the job of administration with much the same "parent problem" that Waller suggests. We might dispute the intensity and seeming irreconcilability of this conflict that Waller describes, but we cannot challenge its existence.

There are many explanations for the seeming distrust that administrators and parents sometimes have of each other. Professional insecurity on the part of school people is only one explanation. Waller correctly notes that parents and school personnel may have different interests. In our own studies we have seen some of these different, though not always conflicting, interests at work. We saw, for example, the high school principal who wanted to integrate special education students as a way of building the positive reputation of his school. We observed another administrator who viewed integration as just another administrative headache, one more special interest with which to contend. Naturally, parents care little about administrator's problems. They want quality services for their sons and daughters. Another explanation for the ongoing tensions between school administrators and parents is the ambiguity of education. What is good education? How do you know when you have achieved quality programming? There are so many theories of learning, so many styles of teaching, so many curricula from which to choose, who can say what is most appropriate? Perhaps if educational practice were less ambiguous it would be easier to sell to parents.

Still another explanation, not unrelated to those we have already mentioned, is that educational administrators know how to manage schools internally—they can negotiate with their own staff, build support in the schools for particular policies or actions—but are less skilled in constituency building with parents or, for that matter, with the public. It is instructive to note the remarkable similarity between this recent finding and Waller's, except that now, the professional insecurity may be masked behind claims of professional competence:

> One must recognize how convention stands in the way [of administrator/ community sharing in decision making] . . . how prevalent is the image of the expert whose training and knowledge are essential to formulating policy- and decision-making. How, then, can the professional justify sharing responsibility in such matters? Why should the educational manager go along with policies and decisions with which he or she is not in full agreement? Of course, within the schools, the principals (and other school administrators) have had to negotiate with the constituencies. But no amount of expertise working with and between teachers, principals, assistant superintendents, school social workers and psychologists, et cetera, has produced any comparable expertise on a similar scale with external constituencies. (Sarason, 1981, p. 52)

While the criticism of administrators as poor constituency builders rings true, we observed numerous programs in which administrators and staff appeared to have excellent relations with parents. We tried to understand what factors characterized these positive examples. In our chapter on parents we discuss examples of school practices that can enhance parent/school relations. In this chapter we examine a few important principles by which district-level administrators can ensure positive, productive interaction with parents.

Administrators who speak positively of parents have good working relations with them. In part, they credit their own favorable attitudes toward parents to their personal interactions—for example, by frequent communication with parents at public meetings, over the phone, and in program-development/program-planning task forces. Those who have positive feelings for parents have initiated interaction with parents; this feature contrasts markedly with the practice of many administrators whose only interaction with parents seemed to be when parents wanted to complain about something. In several major urban districts, we observed or heard about parents working alongside school district staff in developing community-based vocational programs, public school programs for severely and profoundly disabled students, and preschool programs. We also noted, however, that administrators who had the most frequent and deep working relations with parents not only had multiple strategies for promoting interaction, they also had a sense of what it means to be the parent of a child with a disability. They knew, for example, that being a parent may mean

- Watching friends slip away because they do not know what to say, or because they say the wrong thing so often
- Watching your child not have other children to play with in the community
- Seeing your own social life severely diminished because so much of your energy goes to caring for your disabled child
- Experiencing a near absence of community support services such as baby-sitters; day care; sympathetic, understanding, and supportive health care; transportation; and recreation
- Spending countless hours being a "handicapped parent," fighting for the basic services such as physical therapy, speech therapy, assistance in the development of prostheses and aids
- Constantly being on stage before the world, as people, strangers and friends alike, give unsolicited advice about how the parent might try to help the disabled son or daughter
- Begging for assistance when it is not available as a matter of right
- Realizing that there are rarely program or service options, just a single program or service available for disabled students

But some administrators had an even more vivid understanding and appreciation of the parent experience. Here, for example, is what one administrator told us about several families:

We have a couple of families whose kids just weren't sleeping at night. The kids were getting up and walking around the house destroying things. The parents weren't sleeping. It really becomes a question of would they close the door and not let the kid out of the room and go through the screaming, the kid taking apart the room, in order to try to get the kid to learn to stay? I think the parents have made so many compromises because of the sort of degree of their kid's disability that a lot of times it is really hard to do what you have to do to see some progress. So you give in to the kid's rigidity. You give in.

We have a kid whose mother, for years every day, rain, sleet, or snow, followed the kid on an hour-long walk in the fields in their backyard in exactly the same path, on exactly the same schedule. He did it and he would tantrum enormously if she varied from the schedule in any way. He also was used to being fed at four o'clock when he got home from school. When our parent worker approached the family about the possibility of his learning to have dinner with the family, the mother just panicked because she could not imagine that she could handle how upset he would be to have to gradually extend the time. You would have had to do it over a period of time. She would have had to feed him alone later and later until she got to the point where he was then going to eat at the regular dinner hour and at the table with everyone else. They would have had to tolerate how difficult he is at the table and his eating habits, and they would have had to handle changing their patterns too. It was a toss-up of what the gains are with something like that. They ended up not doing it. He still eats at four thirty in the afternoon, three years later. But he now eats with utensils.

It is quite obvious that this administrator feels the staff have expert knowledge that is essential to share. Yet, this administrator also correctly assumes that in order to share information and to develop an effective instructional program for students, it is important to understand the family context.

The typical school district administrator cannot possibly know such specific information about each child or family. The bureaucratic demands of the position make that impossible. But an administrator can make an effort to discover the experiences of one or several families with disabled children. These few examples will "ground" the administrator in the family experience enough to know the compelling value of building constituencies, of initiating with and responding to parents.

Administrators who emphathized and truly seemed to understand the parent experience had no problem understanding the potential benefits of working closely with parents and of respecting parents' rights to challenge professional judgments. A parent whom we interviewed reported to us that he observed a school administrator and teaching staff providing an orientation to student teachers. The administrator remarked: "We have a very important policy here. We treat parents with respect. Parents know a fantastic amount about their children. They want to help their kids. And they can be a superb resource for us. If a parent asks us questions about the program, it is our responsibility to provide clear, concise, understandable answers."

In a school district where the superintendent meets monthly with a parent advisory group, a parent complained, "You set up these teacher inservice days, send notices home to us telling us that our children will be off from school that day for teacher inservice, but you don't even tell us the subject of the inservice. We'd like to know. We'd like to be convinced that this is important." The superintendent promised, immediately, that in the future parents would receive notes telling them of the inservice content. Some districts invite parents to help plan inservices and encourage parents to participate where appropriate.

Many districts have specific policies for informing parents of their children's rights under education laws. Some districts publish parent rights handbooks; others distribute rights materials developed by state education departments or by private groups. Administrators who provide easy-to-understand information about parent rights do so with the knowledge that if parents see them promoting legal rights material, they are less likely to perceive the administrators as "trying to hide something" or as trying to keep all of the power to themselves.

Some administrators involve parents in planning and hiring committees. Parents do not want to sit on committees that have no power. And parents do not want token committee membership. However, we observed administrator/parent task forces in several districts planning new programs for deaf students, for vocational education to serve severely disabled students, and for mainstreaming programs with moderately retarded students. The parents were present in numbers, at least a third, and sometimes more than a half of the committee members. In several schools and school districts, administrators invited parents of students with disabilities to play a major role in screening and interviewing finalists for top-level special education positions. One school had parents on each hiring committee for teacher openings.

Predicting Problems

When lawyers take a case to trial they have as one of their goals that there be no surprises in the courtroom. Thus, they depose witnesses for the opposition, they prepare their own witnesses, and they analyze all of the possible courtroom scenarios that they can possibly imagine. Good administrators attempt much the same strategy when they introduce a major new initiative. They analyze possible opposition, they try to formulate ways of meeting the opposition's challenges, they secure allies, they develop evidence to buttress their view, they determine ways of responding to situations that may arise which could threaten the goal of integration. In order to predict the problems that may arise, they poll their staffs for their ideas, they examine past problems that arise repeatedly, they talk to administrators in other districts, they read about organizational dynamics, and they regularly inquire of themselves, "What are the most difficult challenges that could occur?"

THE CASE OF DEINSTITUTIONALIZATION FOR EDUCATION

In this section of the chapter we present leadership strategies by which administrators can promote the fullest possible integration for students who typically have been the last to benefit from integration. It is instructive to examine a single problem area of integration that presents several of the major barriers (jurisdictional, administrative, and political) and strategies that administrators have employed to resolve it. We take the case of educating institutionalized children and youth.

Institutionalized children and youth are perhaps the least served category of students covered under Public Law 94–142. Students who live in mental-health and mental-retardation facilities are often denied appropriate programming and, in numerous documented cases, denied an education altogether. Yet disabled students who reside in public and private institutions have the same educational rights as their peers in the community. By definition, students in institutions pose a dilemma. They live in segregated, disabled-only environments. Yet they are entitled to services in the least restrictive settings possible and appropriate. The protections contained in P.L. 94–142 apply to all students with handicapping conditions. Furthermore, Section 504, the antidiscrimination clause of the Rehabilitation Act of 1973, explicitly requires that school-aged persons who are institutionalized because of a disability be provided with an appropriate education. Like their noninstitutionalized peers, they are entitled to an appropriate education and related services, due-process protections, placement in the least restrictive environment, and other benefits specified in federal law.

Fulfilling the educational rights of institutionalized children raises difficult and complex questions. Where should programs be located? Who should operate them? How should educational programs be coordinated with other services? Yet if we can answer these questions, if we can help these students achieve integration, then we will have truly begun to overcome the formidable barriers to universal integration. At a small but growing number of sites across the nation, institutionalized students are attending *regular public schools* in the company of both their noninstitutionalized and nonhandicapped peers.

Policy

Sound programmatic and administrative principles support this thrust:

- In accord with state deinstitutionalization efforts, the populations of public institutions are declining (Scheerenberger, 1982). In addition, the average age at most institutions is increasing as fewer children and youth are admitted.
- Historically, public institutions have been unable to fund, recruit, and retain qualified professional staff. Today, even well-financed institutions face critical staff shortages in professional services.
- Like their counterparts living in the community, institutionalized students are entitled to placement in the least restrictive environment (Gilhool and Stutman, 1978). Segregated institutional programs cannot afford opportunities for interaction with nonhandicapped students in educational, extracurricular, and nonacademic activities.
- Public school placement aids in the transition from institution to community for students who will eventually be placed in noninstitutional settings.
- Since the passage of P.L. 94–142, local school districts have become increasingly experienced and sophisticated in educating students with severe disabilities, which form a large segment of the institutional population.
- Placement in local schools provides a break in the monotony of institutional life as well as diversified life experiences.
- Current educational approaches for the severely handicapped, the majority of children and youth institutionalized, emphasize the importance of teaching *functional life skills* in *normal* vocational, domestic, recreational, and community environments (Brown, Wilcox, Sontag, Vincent, Dodd, and Gruenewald, 1977; Sailor, Wilcox, and Brown, 1980). Thus, institutions are ill-equipped to provide severely disabled students with the skills necessary to participate in the wider society.
- Locating responsibility with educational agencies eliminates inefficient parallel administrative structures between educational systems and mental-health and mental-retardation systems. Yet implementation requires

careful planning (Arkell, Thomason, and Haring, 1980; Blatt, Bogdan, Biklen, and Taylor, 1977).
• The transition of institutions from custodial to programmatically oriented facilities has been painstakingly slow and, according to some commentators, is an impossible process (Blatt, McNally, and Ozolins, 1980; Bogdan, Taylor, deGrandpre, and Haynes, 1974; Taylor and Bogdan, 1980; Wolfensberger, 1975).

Residency

State laws and regulations must place responsibility for educating institutionalized students with the school districts in which facilities are located. Several states already have enacted laws which specify that for educational purposes, a child is considered a resident of the school district surrounding an institution. In those instances in which a school district can demonstrate that placement of all institutionalized students in its programs would result in overconcentration, state laws and regulations can provide for a temporary waiver of this requirement.

If favorable state policies do not exist, local administrators may need to seek special permissive legislation or formal interagency agreements at the state level.

Funding

Who should pay for the education of institutionalized students in local schools? Surely, it would be unfair and unwise to expect local school districts themselves to fund these services. In some states, fiscal responsibility for the costs of educating these children is assumed by the state education agency or mental retardation/developmental disabilities or mental health agency. Recently, one major midwestern public school system educated 102 students from a local institution for the mentally retarded in regular schools within the district. The school district receives funds from "sending" districts. That is, the district at the time of institutionalization or the parents' current district is responsible for paying for the education of institutionalized students in local school districts under a "charge-back" policy. Again, if such mechanisms do not currently exist, local administrators will need to seek special legislation or state level interagency agreements.

Transportation

The lack of clear-cut responsibility for providing and funding transportation interferes with the placement of institutionalized children in local schools. At a local school in one state, for example, the special education teacher transports students back and forth from the institution during hours in which the students should be receiving instruction. In another state, the mental retardation department is responsible for transportation costs even though the instructional costs are borne by educational agencies. Since transportation is considered a related service under P.L. 94–142, state regulations and policies should place responsibility for transportation with the agencies responsible for providing and funding instruction.

Attitudes

Prejudicial attitudes toward institutionalized students act as a strong barrier to educating them in local schools in many communities. These attitudes take many forms and reflect many factors. First, there is a tendency in some districts to view institutionalized residents as "the state's children," unwelcome refugees who will drain local resources. Yet these children were born and belong in typical communities. Second, owing to understaffing and institutional practices, institutionalized students may be characterized by an unkempt and disheveled appearance, including baggy, ill-fitting clothes, haphazard grooming, and poor personal hygiene. Finally, in many communities, there is a strong though unfounded fear of contagion from so-called hepatitis B carriers among institutionalized persons. The rights of students classified as hepatitis B carriers have been the subject of federal court cases, the most definitive one relating to ex-Willowbrook residents (*NYSARC v. Carey*).

In the Willowbrook case, Judge John Bartels considered the Board of Education's decision to exclude and then segregate ex-Willowbrook residents classified as hepatitis B carriers. Based on the advice of the local department of health, the Board of Education proposed the creation of segregated programs for forty-eight mentally retarded children identified as hepatitis B carriers. After reviewing the testimony of experts on both sides of the controversy and information from the Center for Disease Control of the U.S. Public Health Service (which stressed the importance of avoiding placing unwarranted limitations or restrictions on retarded carriers of the virus), Judge Bartels upheld the right of these students to placement alongside other students as mandated by P.L. 94–142 and Section 504 of the Rehabilitation Act of 1973. In doing so, he dismissed the unproven risk of contagion from hepatitis B:

> Without requiring that the Board clearly demonstrate existence of significant health risk, we cannot countenance depriving these retarded children of the benefits to be gained by association with other children, handicapped and non-handicapped, nor can we permit any action which, by its stigmatizing consequences, would irreparably disrupt their educational development. (*NYSARC v. Carey*)

Clearly, the integration of institutionalized students in community schools requires special efforts to overcome prejudicial attitudes toward these students held by teachers, school board members, other students, parents, and others. These efforts include sensitization sessions for students; presentations before faculty, school board, and parent meetings; the development of informational fact sheets and educational materials (especially on hepatitis B); and strategies to assure that students' clothing and personal appearances do not draw unnecessary attention to them (for example, assigning teacher aides to help prepare students for school, communicating with institutional staff).

Preparation

In one district the administrators initiated a series of preprogram activities designed to introduce the program to the disabled students, parents, the community, students in the school where the deinstitutionalized students would attend, and to school officials. These activities included the following: the head teacher visited prospective students and their staff or parents; the teacher described the program to institutional staff and arranged for staff and parent visits to the classrooms where the students would attend; the teacher provided the school superintendent a list of ten school districts in the state and other areas of the country that had integrated severely handicapped students into regular public schools; and the teacher prepared a slide/tape presentation for the PTA and for nondisabled students on the goals of the program and the students who would participate in it. The principal of the school in which the program was located said he received no negative reactions from the community or from anyone else concerning the new program.

Coordination

The placement of institutionalized students in local schools requires clear-cut coordination mechanisms. The roles and responsibilities of state and local agencies for providing, funding, and monitoring educational services must be spelled out clearly in interagency agreements.

Local school districts must identify the number and educational needs of students to be placed in their schools. Further, school districts need to identify space in local schools; hire and train teachers; obtain educational materials; prepare regular educators, parents, students and others for the arrival of institutionalized students; and work out other logistical problems. In the midwest city noted earlier, students from the institution were phased into the school system gradually, with the number increasing from 20 to 102 over a three-year period.

Specific staff members should be designated to coordinate the placement of institutionalized students in community schools. In the case noted above, the school district employs one half-time administrative assistant and one full-time diagnostic teacher solely to coordinate the transition from the institution to the local schools. Their responsibilities include planning, individual education program planning, student evaluation, and liaison between institutional and school district staff.

Finally, specific strategies must be employed to insure open communication and carry-over between the institution and the school program. A special deinstitutionalization project in a New England state which serves three institutionalized students in an integrated public school program, has developed a series of communication strategies between the institution and school staff: communication notebooks sent back and forth with the student; daily phone contact; joint participation in evaluation and individual program plan meetings; regular meetings to review student progress and program revisions; videotaping students in school for institutional staff; and preparing charts to be used by institutional staff in recording students' behavior at the institution. Administrators can implement each of these strategies before a program ever gets started.

Individual Education Programs

While institutional staff should be involved in developing and reviewing student IEP's, the local school district must assume ultimate responsibility for this process.

Parent Involvement

Since institutionalization often is accompanied by a break in family ties, schools must make special efforts to involve parents of institutionalized students in educational decision making. See our chapter on parents for specific strategies. Of course, for those students whose parents are unable or unwilling to become involved in educational decision making, surrogate parents must be assigned as mandated by P.L. 94–142. While few states have successfully enlisted surrogate parents for institutionalized children and youth, a growing body of literature describes effective strategies for recruiting, training, and supervising surrogates (see, for example, Vermont Surrogate Parent Program, n.d.; Georgia Learning Resources System and National Association of State Directors of Special Education, 1980; and Thomas, 1980).

It is also important that parents and surrogates of institutionalized children have access to the same due-process procedures as parents of children living in the community. In one state, the directors of institutions serve as "impartial hearing officers," an arrangement that violates P.L. 94–142.

Dispersal

Institutionalized students should be assigned throughout schools and classes within a district. Some of the major benefits of public school placement are undermined by congregation of institutionalized students in a single class or school. Dispersal of institutionalized students into classes and programs in each school or a large number of schools protects against stigmatization of these students and provides opportunities for them to be involved in school activities with their disabled and nondisabled peers.

CONCLUSION

The school district administrator's role in mainstreaming, while quite different from that of teachers or even principals, is no less important in the long run. Administrators can set the context within which integration unfolds. In this chapter we have outlined effective strategies that a strong administrator can employ to promote integration. At the outset, the administrator can apply basic decision principles and analysis. This involves making an inventory of who influences particular types of decisions, on what basis, and to what ends. It means developing conscious plans for change, for example "floating" trial balloons, linking integration to other popular issues (e.g., saving the district from having to close more schools), providing rewards to people who support the integration effort, building support for a decision by appealing to diverse constituencies (e.g., teachers, principals, and parents).

At the same time, the effective district-level administrator approaches the task of integration with a thorough understanding of factors that traditionally militate against it. The barriers are technological, attitudinal, jurisdictional, administrative, political, architectural, economic, personnel, logistical, legal, motivational, and what we have called idiosyncratic.

Leadership strategies aimed specifically at facilitating integration go beyond general principles of organizational change by directly addressing each of the barriers. Specifically, administrative strategies include: a policy of normalization (normal patterns), continuity in location of special education programs, replacing jargon with ordinary language, utilization of a functional curriculum model, keeping track of progress of students and programs, grouping students appropriately by age, integrating students "widely" rather than congregating special programs and students in a few schools, promoting an ethic of equality among students, minimizing the use of labels for students and programs, learning about the nature of change by listening to the people primarily responsible for the changes (e.g., teachers and support staff), articulating a moral and legal commitment to integration, starting integration by planning carefully, abolishing financial incentives to segregate disabled students, providing adequate training for teachers, effectively involving parents, understanding what parents' lives with their disabled sons and daughters are like, and predicting the kinds of problems that arise when a district integrates special and regular education.

Finally, we have applied the principles and strategies for change to a difficult form of integration, namely providing schooling to children and youth who live in institutions. This type of integration has proven difficult because it calls into play so many of the barriers to integration (e.g. jurisdictional, administrative, personnel, economic, logistical, attitudinal, and legal. But for this same reason this issue provided an excellent opportunity to "problem-solve." The specific strategies noted in our discussion of educational deinstitutionalization, as with all of the examples in this book, were drawn from school districts' actual experiences.

5

Parents

DOUGLAS BIKLEN AND STANFORD J. SEARL, JR.

I really do believe that parents do know their kids better than the teacher. If the goal of education, particularly with special kids, is to get them to fit into the world and function, leaving parents out, I think you are missing a whole lot in the program. *Loyola Quinn, parent*

THE PARENT'S PERSPECTIVE IS DIFFERENT

This chapter is about parents. It is also about teachers and administrators, and parents' interaction with them. In the previous chapters we have identified key issues that touch each of the groups discussed (e.g., principals, teachers, district administrators). In the chapter on teachers, we explored mainstreaming and all that it means from the perspective of teachers. In the chapter on administration we looked at what mainstreaming means to principals. We also examined how administrators respond to the many challenges that mainstreaming poses. Similarly, in the first chapter, we attempted to isolate basic principles that special education directors, superintendents, state special education directors, and others can employ to promote mainstreaming. In this chapter we focus on the parents' perspectives. How do parents feel about mainstreaming? What is it that parents want from schools? How much interaction with teachers is good? What do parents dislike most about how school personnel respond to them? What do parents need to know in order to be effective advocates for their sons and daughters? What do school personnel need to know about parents?

By way of answering or, at least, exploring these questions, we have looked primarily at what we call the "parent issues" from parents' perspectives. To be sure, parents, teachers, and administrators do not always see eye to eye. In fact, they often disagree. Thus, we make no pretense at trying to discover a "true" perspective on integration. We firmly believe there is no one correct perspective. Rather, we believe that each perspective on integration is legitimate and important. Each is worth understanding. Similarly we have witnessed and will describe markedly contrasting styles of parent interactions with schools. We explore how schools can make parents feel more welcome in schools. We also describe strategies that parents sometimes employ to force change on unwilling schools and school districts. In the following pages we share what we have learned about parents' perspectives and strategies.

ONE PARENT'S CAMPAIGN FOR INTEGRATION

You could think of it as consciousness raising. As we were forced to start scrambling for information [about how best to educate our daughter], it became clearer to me the meaning and importance of "least restrictive environment." I would have to say that I was not aware of it previously.

So speaks Loyola Quinn, a mother who has become a strong advocate of mainstreaming. She believes that her daughter Bridget, who has multiple disabilities, can benefit from some interaction with nondisabled students. She wants her school program located in a regular elementary school. In fact, she believes so firmly in this goal that she and her husband filed a request for an impartial hearing in order to demand it.

Eventually, the Quinns' appeal was dismissed by the commissioner of education in their state, but only after the commissioner encouraged the local school district to plan for providing Bridget a program in a regular school. A year after the hearing, Bridget attended a special program in a regular school where she had opportunities to interact with nondisabled students. Later, when her home district did not establish an integrated program, she was back in a segregated school.

The Quinns asked us to consult on their daughter's case just at the time we were beginning our study funded by the National Institute of Education. We became fascinated by, and very much involved in this case because it raised many of the issues which we intended to study. The record of Bridget Quinn's appeal for integration suggests how a great many parents think about mainstreaming and why they think it is important. While relatively few parents initiate impartial hearings on their children's behalf, many share Loyola Quinn's commitment to integration for their sons and daughters. We present some of the testimony from the impartial hearing in order to explain this perspective.

In his review of her appeal, the commissioner of education described Bridget's disabilities:

> The nature of her handicapping conditions includes severe mental retardation and physical disabilities. Her language skills are pre-verbal and are characterized by the use of syllables, laughter, and babbling. Physically, she has considerably more difficulty with her gross motor skills than with her fine motor skills. She is able to crawl and to stand upright using a support for balance. Her self-help skills are minimal; she is able to drink from a bottle but unable to use eating utensils and is not toilet-trained. Socially, the child responds to attention especially when given individually. There is some indication in her most recent individualized educational program that she has recently shown increased interest in her peers and has begun to interact with them. (*Loyola Quinn v. Niskayuna Central School District, 1979*)

For the first year of her schooling, Bridget attended a special class in a state developmental center. She then moved to a special class in a special school operated by a special intermediate school district. When she entered this program, Bridget's parents protested the fact that it was segregated and called for active parent involvement.

Loyola Quinn tells why she feels teacher/parent dialogue is so important:

> One of the things we hear a great deal is that our children need intensive remediation. If you can accept that idea of intensive programming, then regardless of how chock-full the five-hour school day is, it is still not going to totally meet her needs. Now, if we are going to work with Bridget at home to reinforce what she learns at school, and not to completely work at cross-purposes, then we must understand the techniques that are being used. We absolutely have to have a really in-depth understanding of what the professionals are doing with this child. Then we can do our best to treat her in a similar manner. We can try to reinforce what they are doing. It can be a cooperative thing.

On the integration issue, Loyola Quinn wants an integrated school, but believes that interaction between severely disabled and nondisabled students must be well planned:

I have observed Bridget for six years and I have watched her curiosity grow about where she is. As a very young child she wasn't very curious, and she was limited to whatever was around her. As she was able to get up and move, she began to be interested in those kinds of things that she could reach. She reacts and interacts with our other children, who are seven and three. She knows particular people who come into our house on a regular basis. You can tell the difference between someone she knows and someone that she doesn't know.

Because she is interested in observing her environment, I am concerned with having her have the most exposure to the ebb and flow of all the things that comprise a normal environment, the most important of which would, of course, be her school setting.

I think even sounds like the noisy hallways or the hubbub of the cafeteria that were mentioned this morning have a certain stimulation and they are the kinds of things that she will have to get used to if she is going to live outside of a very restrictive environment all her life.

I also believe that those children who would be attracted to Bridget much in the way any of us make friends—some children perhaps will not be able to interact with Bridget, this is the normal child—but I do believe that those kids who have those sympathies and interests will then have an opportunity to seek out some kind of formalized contact, which would again have to be handled very sensitively by the school staff. There would have to be a well-planned interaction between these children much in the same way as I understand in the normal classroom the older students come in and help younger children with reading lessons. I think that if it were well planned and well supervised I could see no reason why an older child couldn't come in and do some of the simple tasks with Bridget occasionally, that kind of thing.

There is no reason that Bridget couldn't have her lunch-feeding program in a school cafeteria. She could not have music appreciation stimulation, singing in the music room. . . . If, indeed, they do have visual aids, they could do this in the media center of any school as well as they could do it at [her present school]. They could use the gym for large motor activities.

We want opportunities for modeling, . . . Bridget can see, she can hear, and those things I believe that she sees and hears will be the kinds of things that she will imitate. . . . Much of Bridget's development has come in the same way that it comes in a normal child. Not all that she has learned has been taught to her. . . . She has done much under her own steam, if you will. . . . She would respond to all the kinds of stimulation and observations,

perhaps at a much slower rate than a normal child will, but she would do
this. . . . Unless we give her that opportunity, we will never know whether
she can do it.

When Loyola Quinn speaks about integrating Bridget into a regular
school, we can hear her confidence. She has specific reasons why she
thinks integration would benefit Bridget. She speaks of getting used to
noise, of watching other students at mealtime, of noticing how nondisabled students dress and walk, of participating in some of the normal
routines of school life. She does not want to whitewash Bridget's obviously
significant disabilities. But at the same time she asks that Bridget not be
segregated unnecessarily.

Loyola Quinn has thought a lot about her daughter's development.
Like so many parents of children with disabilities, she recognized that
she needed to become an expert on many aspects of her daughter's needs
in order to advocate effectively for her. To recall her own words, "we
were forced to start scrambling for information." During the first several
years of Bridget's schooling, Loyola Quinn schooled herself on theories
and methods of special education. She developed an analysis of what
would be in Bridget's interests. That knowledge, that sense of what
Bridget needed, was critical to her ability to speak effectively on Bridget's
behalf.

"I'M NO CHARITY CASE"

How would you like it if you were constantly made to feel that your
son or daughter's education was an unnatural burden on the taxpayer?
How would you feel if you could never be sure where your children's
school program would be located from year to year, in the neighborhood
school where all the area students attend or perhaps in a school across
town? How would you feel if your child's class always seemed to be
located at the end of the farthest corridor or in the least appealing basement
classroom? How would you feel if the Parents/Teachers Organization
never seemed to be concerned with the issues that were most pressing to
you and to your children? How would you feel if other parents sometimes
told you that they worried that your child was slowing down their child's
educational progress?

For most parents, such questions would never arise. They believe
their sons and daughters *are* entitled to their education. Their schooling

poses no special burden to the taxpayer. They feel their children have a right to continuity in schooling, to have their program located in the same place for several years at a time. They find that the PTO *does* concern itself with their concerns. And they rarely, if ever, hear other parents suggest that their children will slow down educational progress. Yet, parents of students with disabilities experience such things regularly. To have a child with a disability is to know prejudice. No matter how well the schools respond to a student's needs, no matter how well intentioned the staff, friends, and acquaintances, no parent can completely escape the prejudices imposed on children and youth with disabilities. Of course it is our goal to end such indignities, such prejudices, such discrimination. But in the meantime, parents of students with disabilities have grown accustomed to coping with prejudice and to combatting it at every turn.

Ironically, even heartfelt sympathy sometimes makes parents of disabled students feel isolated, different, and ostracized. Every teacher in the field of special education has heard many times over, from friends and acquaintances, the phrases: "Oh, so you're in special education. I don't know how you do it; I could never do it." "Is it depressing?" 'It's so good of you to give up your life for them." "You must be so patient." Teachers generally feel that such comments reflect a lack of awareness about who disabled people are and of what they are capable. When someone says these things to you, you feel like they are saying, "You're a different kind of person, a special person: you're not like the rest of us." At the same time, such comments create a distance between those speaking and those to whom they are spoken. Parents encounter the same kinds of statements: "Oh, I'm so sorry for you." "Will he ever be independent?" "Is there any hope for her?" "I don't know how you do it." "I think I'd institutionalize mine if I ever had one." Such comments, however well intentioned, construct a gulf between speaker and parent. A parent who hears such comments time and again begins to feel as if his or her child is being transformed from a person into an object, a stereotype.

Unfortunately, such comments reflect attitudes and practices deeply rooted in society at large. Ironically, they surface most frequently in some of the organizations that are dedicated to helping disabled people, namely charities. For years, children and youth with disabilities have been the focus of massive charity drives. Such fund-raising efforts exist in nearly every local community and in many public and private schools. In recent years parents have become more and more resistant to participating in such fund raising. Many have been openly critical of charity drives for the disabled. Again, like the well-intentioned comments noted above, parents feel that charity fund-raising techniques tend to stereotype their sons and daughters. Some people believe that charity's real benefactors are the politicians and entertainment stars who, through their charitable activities, are seen by the public as "doing good." Others question the images that charities promote: of bright-eyed young people seeking gifts with their smiles, or their highly visible apparatus such as an oversized wheelchair or leg brace, or their sad, vacant looks that plead for pity. Many parents wonder why basic human services must be funded through the elaborate and often risky fund-raising gimmicks like walkathons, telethons, auctions, benefit concerts, corporate matching campaigns, and the like. As television talk-show host Phil Donahue puts it, "We don't have telethons or bikeathons or walkathons for highways or airports; why must we resort to this loosely organized and often unsuccessful Roman circus to raise funds for our children?" (Donahue, 1979, p. 225). So right he is. Charities depend on the popularity of sponsoring stars, the eye-catching allure of fund-raising gimmickery, and other unreliable factors for their success. As such, human services that rely on charity are by their nature fragile and often unreliable. Understandably, parents of students who have disabilities want educational and other basic human services available as a matter of right not as a privilege that depends on a "Roman circus."

What parents want is really quite simple. They want equality for their children. In more specific terms this means they want:

1. The right to have their sons and daughters receive an education at public expense.
2. Continuity in schooling. Parents do not want their children tossed about like political footballs, from one school or program to another depending on where there is space or funding.
3. Real integration in the mainstream of school life. Parents of handi-capped students do not want to feel that their children are attending public school on an experimental basis. They want to feel they have the right to be there, that they are accepted as "regular" members of the school.
4. Parent integration. Parents of students with disabilities want to par-ticipate in school events and activities alongside parents of typical students. They do not want to be made to feel different, unusual, freakish.

5. Their sons and daughters to be treated as individuals and not as stereotypes of "the disabled."
6. Their children to be regarded as assets not burdens. No parent feels good about his or her child's being cast as a burden on the taxpayer or as an impediment to other children's speed of learning. Parents of students with disabilities want other parents, schools, and the public to regard special education and mainstreaming as in the societal interest and not just in the interest of their children.
7. Open dialogue. Parents of students with disabilities want to have people ask them questions about disabilities and about their children's needs. They want people to be willing to learn about disabilities and about their sons and daughters who have disabilities. They do not want people holding them at arm's length with such seemingly kind, but actually hurtful, phrases as "I don't know how you do it. I could never do it."
8. A shared commitment to rooting out prejudice. Parents of disabled students do not generally feel that the mission of rooting out prejudice toward people with disabilities, what we have called "handicapism," is theirs alone. The task of fighting handicapism belongs to all. The goal of equality for people with disabilities should be a goal everyone shares.
9. An informed school. Parents often know more about the rights of disabled students than do many school personnel. While most schools have a few staff who are well informed, parents frequently feel that their children suffer from a general lack of awareness on the part of many staff about disability rights, about the experience of having a disability, and about ongoing efforts locally and nationally to overcome barriers to equality. Parents want schools to become informed.
10. Cooperation. While many parents have to resort to confrontation tactics in order to secure needed services for their children, most want to work cooperatively with schools. Parents want schools to know that they have much to offer the schools.

CAN PARENTS AND TEACHERS GET ALONG?

Parents and teachers do not always get along. We have met teachers who complain, "The problem is that too many parents just don't get involved, they just don't care." On the other hand, we have also heard the complaint that "some parents get too involved; they want to control everything; they don't think we (teachers) have anything to offer." Similarly, we have heard parents express their distrust of teachers and schools. One parent put it this way. "Any school is only as good as the people that are teaching in it. You have to do what I do with his teachers; you go in and look them over and size them up. I do the same thing with my other children's teachers. . . . I size them up and make any changes right away." Even if these teachers and parents are not representative, we can assume that at least some of the time some parents and teachers are separated by a gulf of mistrust, skepticism, and hostility.

The problem is understandable. One analyst of parent/school relations has suggested that parents feel at once intimidated by authoritative school officials, ground down by the schools' bureaucratic ways, or subconsciously awed by the image of schools which they remember from their childhood:

> Most parents stand in awe of school people and systems because schools represent our childhood images of authority and mystifying expertise. We are all products of school systems and we still retain a number of childlike school behaviors based on the old rules: "Stand in line," "No gum chewing," "No talking out of turn." The school building brings out these old feelings and behaviors in practically everyone who doesn't work in a school. School people who feel most secure in authoritarian roles tend to exploit this habitual response to shore up their status with almost everyone who is not a regular part of the system. They may use a commanding tone of voice, keep people waiting in the outer office or halls, require silence as you walk the corridors, and generally treat parents as children and intruders. They make it clear that everyone in the building has a particular place, and the parent's place is that of the child. (Cutler, 1981, p. 33)

Another common feeling of parents is that they are simply forgotten, left out, not valued. For these and perhaps other reasons, many parents feel relatively powerless.

Ironically, many teachers also feel powerless. While most teachers view parents as helpful resources, they also feel, albeit sometimes unconsciously, that parents can threaten their autonomy and their professionalism. When parents begin to make demands on them, to question their teaching approach or to recommend one, to offer unsolicited suggestions or to ask something special, teachers feel that their territory has been invaded. After all, the classroom is the place where teachers have traditionally had their greatest power.

Is this seemingly unresolvable conflict resolvable? Can teachers and parents work together? Can they view their interests as compatible? Obviously, many teachers and parents have found a way to work out the potential conflict. In schools where parent involvement has been successful certain conditions related to parent participation seem always to be present:

- The school has a policy of promoting parent involvement (for all parents, that is for those with disabled and nondisabled children).
- Parent involvement takes many forms, ranging from the informal (e.g., parent/teacher phone calls, parent assistance on field trips) to the formal (parent involvement in individual education programs, parents/teachers organizations).
- Teacher interviews of parents about student abilities, needs, and difficulties.
- Ongoing system by which teachers and parents can communicate with each other.
- Periodic formal parent/teacher conferences.
- Parent involvement in planning new programs.
- Availability of school facilities for parent meetings.
- Involvement of parents in decision-making circles within the school.
- Provision by the school to the parents of specific, clear information about student and parent rights.
- Combined parent/teacher efforts at community education about the needs of disabled students and the ways in which a community can help to integrate disabled students.
- Parent-to-parent strategies (e.g., encouraging "old-timer" parents to help "up-and-coming" parents).
- Availability of special education, parent education, and self-help information (e.g. magazines, books and newsletters) for parents.

SCHOOLS THAT INTEGRATE PARENTS

When a major school district in the southwestern part of the United States proposed to integrate severely handicapped high-school-age students into a regular high school and close its segregated special school, parents of these handicapped students offered fierce resistance. Many feared for their children's safety. Some believed their children's education would be diluted. Some asked, "Why close a program that we know works?"

District officials thought integration of these handicapped students would enhance their education: integration provides better programs and more interaction with nondisabled students; handicapped students would benefit by being served in a building designed for their age group and by observing nonhandicapped students as role models.

The parents remained unconvinced. They appealed the district's decision to the federal Office for Civil Rights. Even when their appeal failed, the parents continued to resist. They began a defense fund to finance a court battle to prevent the closing of the segregated school.

The district proceeded to close the special facility and to integrate the high school. At the same time, district officials tried to allay parent concerns. The district used various strategies, including the following, to win the parents' support:

- Administrators met regularly with parents to discuss and seek advice on plans for integration.
- Administrators stated their integration goals candidly.
- Administrators remained open to the possibility that the integrated program might prove *not* to be the most appropriate placement for these severely handicapped high school students.
- Parents were encouraged to visit integrated schools.
- An administrator was assigned at each integrated site to be responsible for making integration work—this included maintaining an ongoing dialogue with parents.

By the end of the first year of integration, parents who had originally opposed the program had become its strong supporters. They donated their defense fund to the school to support the new program. So far not one major negative incident has occurred at the high school between severely handicapped and nondisabled students. The segregated facility has been sold for a private technical vocational institute. Parent initiative in lobbying for new programs often proves effective, and many school officials realize this. Sometimes administrators *seek* parent help. A school system in Alaska, for example, regularly enlists parents to help explain to school boards and the public the kinds of programs that are needed.

Sometimes parents make the first move. In 1971 some parents of severely handicapped youngsters urged their state to develop a statewide system of service for their children. The parents invited legislators to a breakfast meeting in a church. About one-third of the invited legislators came. The speaker was Dr. Eric Schopler, an advocate in the education of children with autism. The others who attended were about fifteen parents and their children, brought so the legislators could personally see children with autism.

The parents' strategy worked. By making their case vividly and at a human level, the parents secured the support of the legislators. The state legislature passed a law that established a statewide system of diagnostic and educational service for all autistic children in the state. Most of these educational programs are provided in regular public schools.

Parents can also play important consultative and decision-making roles in development and planning. In a major Midwest community, the public schools and a university jointly sponsor a task force on curriculum development. Advanced graduate students and teachers staff the task force. This task force on curriculum development meets regularly with parents of severely handicapped students to solicit the parents' ideas about activities for their sons and daughters.

The same district does extensive vocational planning for each severely handicapped student. Again, parents are involved. A vocational "transition specialist" meets with the student's family. Together they discuss possible post-school vocational placements, identify the family's ideas and goals for the student, and plan public school assessment and vocational training that will facilitate a smooth transition for community placement.

Parents at an alternative school that mainstreams severely disabled and nondisabled students visit other schools to explain their integrated school approach to other parents and administrators. Through outreach efforts the parents encourage other schools to begin planning more public school programs for autistic children.

In one rural state, parents work with regular and special educators on regional task forces to integrate severely handicapped students into public school settings. Parents join together with local decision makers (including administrators and teachers) in five task forces. The task forces implement full integration by

- Providing maximum social integration between handicapped and nonhandicapped peers
- Achieving age-appropriate placements in public school settings with nonhandicapped people

- Increasing the use of community-based, functional life skills
- Modifying the IEP and the curriculum
- Providing a more effective transition from educational to vocational programs for the severely handicapped

One well-known statewide public education effort that serves autistic children and youth calls parents co-teachers. Staff members invite parents to observe teachers and other professionals as they work with these students. Then each parent attempts the same teaching exercises. Sometimes these training exercises are videotaped so parents can observe their own teaching. These parent-training sessions take place at a diagnostic center, at school, or in the home.

This concept of parent-as-teacher ensures that parents know the specific nature of their children's educational programs. It also helps parents carry out educational strategies at home that are consistent with those of the school.

Public Law 94–142 (1975) requires that parents have opportunities to provide information about their children in the assessment process and that parents be involved in developing their children's individual education plans.

Many school districts have developed strategies to make the most of parent involvement. Teachers in one educational system interview parents to learn about the student's behavior at home and in the community. They also ask parents what skills they want their sons and daughters to learn. Thus, teachers can learn how the educational program can help improve the students' participation in community and family life.

Teachers at another school visit families in their homes and help parents identify their children's strengths and weaknesses. This process insures that the school programs will be relevant to the children's needs and those of the families.

The school's principal explains what this can mean for a student and his or her family:

We now know more of the right questions to ask. Yesterday we had a case conference on one of our students. After talking with his family, we realized that one thing he needed to learn was to relax and keep quiet during a movie. So we plan to take him into public places more and to some movies. Learning this skill will truly help him to fit in better with his family.

PARENT GROUPS

Many have no names. Some form over a crisis. Some have big budgets. They are all parent groups. In every community we visited we inquired about parent groups. Are there any parent groups in this area? What kinds of groups are they? How many people belong? What have they accomplished? What are they trying to accomplish?

After talking with parents, interviewing parents, looking over written documents from parent groups, and serving as consultants to parent groups, we have concluded that whether large or small, ad hoc and crisis-oriented or firmly established, parent groups tend to fall into one of three types. A few groups do all of the things that most characterize each type, but most lean toward one form or another.

Type One: Consciousness-Raising/Support Groups

In this type of group parents come together on a regular basis to share experiences, to find support, and to discover solutions to the problems they face. In these groups, parents swap "war" stories about encounters with hostile school principals, unsympathetic or, the opposite, pitying neighbors, and others. They share experiences, a process that invariably leads each member of the group to realize that his or her experience is not at all unlike what most other parents of children and youth with disabilities experience. Sometimes they focus on their children's behavior. Other times they talk about society. They discuss incidents that to them typify the kinds of prejudice they feel. Most important perhaps, aside from merely lending an interested ear to each other, parents share strategies for responding to people who have prejudicial attitudes. They share information about which school officials are more responsive to parents.

Some comments from parents who belong to consciousness-raising groups follow. The mother of a child with a learning disability talks about her encounters with prejudice:

When I moved here, I was invited to a bridge club, and I was telling about my children. I said, "Paul has a learning disability." Maude said, "You talk about it? You don't talk about it around here. I'll give you a clue." I said, "Well, do you suppose I shouldn't talk about my daughter's trick knees either?" I couldn't believe it. I think since then some other people have come

out of the closet. With people being able to find other people in the same boat
and working together they are going to get more for their kids.

The parent of a severely disabled child talks about another kind of prejudice:

> Most people, when I tell them Dan is going to public school, say to me,
> "Oh, do you think that's wise?" Sometimes they make me feel horribly
> guilty, like I'm doing something really bad. One woman told me she would
> never let her son go to a public school. "They belong in their own school,"
> she said. I told her, "I was afraid to take the chance at first, but it has worked
> out really well for Dan."

Sometimes they talk about problems with schools:

> I could see Marie was upset coming home from school, but she couldn't
> tell me what was happening. Our communications with school were very
> poor. I would hear from the special education teacher what she was doing,
> but I couldn't find out what was going on in the regular class.

And at other times, parents share their feelings of satisfaction with the
schools:

> Each kid has a little spiral assignment pad in their lunchbox on which
> parents and teachers can communicate with each other around anything that
> they consider an issue. From my standpoint I can give feedback to them. I
> can say, "Look, he really had a bad night. He only slept an hour and a half.
> That may take its toll with you today." They are prepared that way. All the
> kids have notebooks. They are in the boxes every day.

Type Two: Skills-Building Groups

Parents form groups in which they learn how to teach their children,
how to assess the degree of their children's disabilities, how to help their
children overcome their disabilities, and how to use aids, how to secure
funding for the many devices and services they need. Parents form groups
to learn about their legal rights. Parents form groups to learn about various
kinds of programs for children with disabilities. Typically, such groups
invite experts in to provide them with information. In some groups,
members take turns making presentations. One group we learned about

during one of the two studies has a member present a problem that his or her child is having. Then the group combines its knowledge to develop a strategy for overcoming the problem. Another group has developed a structured curriculum for training its members in education rights, the nature of different child assessment procedures, state and local educational policy, skills of giving advice, skills of identifying problems, and skills of negotiating. This group's literature encourages other parents to become involved in the skills-building curriculum: "Remember the first parent/ school meeting about your child that you ever went to?" a brochure begins. "You probably felt nervous, unprepared, even tongue-tied. You may have left with more questions than when you entered. And you probably couldn't remember anyone's name. Lots of other parents feel the same way. But some of us can look back now and say, 'If only I had known then what I do now.' " This parent group helps parents learn what they need to know in order to represent effectively their own children. This is typical of the skills-building type of group.

Type Three: Parent Education/Action Groups

Another type of parent organization devotes itself primarily to advocacy. Such groups develop goals, priorities, and action strategies. One such group we learned about is described in another section of this chapter. It is a group in North Carolina that advocated successfully for a statewide system for providing schooling for autistic children. Another of the programs we observed was the direct product of parent advocacy. Parents of deaf children throughout an urban/suburban county held workshops on parents' rights, filed a lawsuit against several school districts that refused to develop deaf education programs, publicly demanded formation of a countywide planning committee to create deaf education programs, and pursued that goal until programs were begun. We spoke with other advocacy-style parent groups that were lobbying individual school districts to open up and adapt vocational education programs for disabled students. In most cases, such parent groups defined their roles as (1) pressuring for new programs, (1) advocating for greater access to existing ones, and (3) monitoring programs. While the range of strategies available to parent action groups was very broad (e.g., action research, in which they gathered evidence of a problem or recommendations for solutions; litigation; public education through feature and news stories, television appearances, and public forums; lobbying), their principal strategy is negotiating, a topic we cover in some detail in the next section of this chapter.

THE GENTLE ART OF NEGOTIATING

As most parents of children with disabilities will tell you, unless you have the luck of finding an exceptionally open and committed school staff, you have to advocate for your child if you want a quality program. That means you have to be a negotiator. You have to know when to be firm, when to be conciliatory, when to get angry, and when to praise. You have to know what questions to ask, and to whom you should address them. You need to know what is important and how to communicate your interests.

During the course of this study, we have talked with many parents. Most of them expressed satisfaction with their present programs. But nearly all of them offered us hints on how they have been successful in improving their children's programs even when things were not going very well. Rather than hide this side of parent-school relations, we felt it should be presented openly. We met one woman, for example, who had been dissatisfied with the fact that her son had no way to communicate. So she arranged for him to be evaluated by speech pathologists at a medical facility. They recommended augmentative communication technology, in his case an electronic board that he could use for selecting words and creating sentences. With an electronic board he could communicate with his peers and teachers. The school district cited red tape as a reason why it could not pay for the equipment quickly. So the parents sought help from the boy's grandfather. With the $2,300 communicator in hand, the boy began to communicate. These parents continually meet with school officials, put the school officials in touch with the augmentative communication specialists, and pressure for more aggressive use of augmentative communication with their son. Now the school is taking pride in its efforts and success. Meanwhile, the mother has formed a group of parents to advocate for more widespread use of augmentative communication in the schools. The parents surveyed twenty other parents whose youngsters have communication boards. All but one reported that their child's "teacher does not use the communication board that the child has." Then she and another parent asked medical personnel in their state about the resource people they call on when dealing with severely and profoundly disabled children and youth. The parents were disappointed to find that "most of them did not mention parents as resources that they use in their work." The parents speak openly of their findings, using their action research results as evidence that school and human service professionals need to become more responsive to parents and children.

This mother believes that parents have to be willing to speak up. She gave us an example of what she meant. Her son had spent two and one half of his first five years of life in a nursing home. As a result, "he got used to having people around him. When we got him home, I couldn't even go downstairs to do the laundry without him having a fit when I left him." He was the same way in school. So his mother spoke up. "I had it written into his individual education program that he could be left alone for some periods of time during the school day so that he could get used to being independent. And that has worked out very nicely." This is the first time that the school has ever had a severely disabled child. As the mother explained, "At first, they treated him like glass." They were afraid he would get hurt. But since then people have become more relaxed around him. In this case, the parents feel that because they initiated giving advice, they have been able to help the school become more comfortable with their son.

This example typifies the "working out" process that parents and schools experience together, albeit from somewhat different perspectives. Sometimes the parent/staff negotiations or dialogue go smoothly, uneventfully. Other times, tempers flare, interests conflict, and priorities do not match. And most parents know this. They come to expect that the path to educational and other services for their sons and daughters is sometimes bumpy. They also come to know that they must be skilled in order to get the best services for their children. It is not so much that they love parent involvement or parent participation. It is that they regard parent involvement or participation as an essential means of getting for their children what they so dearly need, a good education.

From our discussions with parents and school officials, we discerned the basic principles of negotiating that parents have used when more informal discussion fails:

- *Have a set of principles.* If we have basic principles in which we believe, such as the principle of normalization, the right of equal treatment, the right to be treated as an individual and not as an object, then we always have a way of examining a situation or program and of evaluating it. Only then can we know for what we want to negotiate.

- *Establish goals.* Make lists of all the things we want for our sons and daughters. What is most important? Number each goal in order of importance.
- *Select winnable goals.* Negotiate for the ones that are both important and imminently winnable first. We cannot win every goal immediately, so we need to make choices, recognizing that we can pursue each of the goals in its turn.
- *Be informed.* It may seem unfair, but it is nevertheless necessary, as any parent will confirm, that we have to become somewhat expert on special education and related topics if we want to negotiate effectively on our children's behalf. We noted above that a parent of a severely disabled child had to become informed about augmentative communication. That is just one example. Many parents find themselves poring over state laws, regulations, federal laws, accounts of recent court decisions, new approaches to teaching children and youth with certain disabilities.
- *Know with whom to negotiate.* It is important to determine who has the authority to make certain decisions or take certain actions. It is almost always best to go up the chain of command in an organization (e.g., teacher first, then supervisor or principal, then district official and school board). If we jump right to the top, to the person with the greatest authority, that person will often be reluctant to do anything until consulting with those who actually operate the programs. Also, we lose credibility if we constantly take our issues to the top decision-making circles. Most issues can be resolved at lower levels.
- *Communicate clearly.* Once having identified goals, priorities, and winability, we are ready to negotiate. It helps to be able to communicate the main points clearly and concisely. Lots of parent groups hold their own mock negotiations before going into the real thing. Through such role plays or simulations, we become adept at making our points clearly and convincingly. Several techniques can help: giving good documentation; giving down-to-earth examples of what we mean; stating the human costs of not implementing our plan or accepting our goal; speaking slowly enough so that our ideas can be digested; giving time for those to whom we are speaking to speak back; and staying on our agenda or sequence of points, not allowing ourselves to be taken off

on unrelated or unproductive tangents. Also, we can usually communicate any idea in several different ways, with personal examples, by citing other existing programs or policies similar to what we seek, by offering statistics, by referring to public law and policies and by appealing to common sense.

- *Compromise.* There is rarely much point in compromising on major issues or basic principles (unless you have a plan to achieve implementation of principles over a period of time). But there is no harm in lesser compromise. Negotiations demand compromise. We have to be willing to make deals in order to achieve gains. As long as we do not issue ultimatums and inflexible demands, we can leave room for compromise on both sides, thus making conflict resolution truly possible.

- *Keep on the issues.* Many groups resist advocacy-style negotiations because they do not want to offend a school principal, teacher, or other person with whom they might negotiate. The point is that there is no need to be offensive. If our ideas—that is, what we want for our children and youth—are offensive, then so be it. But we need not offend in the style of our negotiating. We can get emotional, even angry, if it is over the issues. But there is no use in attacking individuals, calling for individuals' resignations, and reducing negotiations to name calling. In fact, if we are the objects of name calling, it is best to point that out and to return the discussion to the issues.

- *Develop a negotiation plan.* Which point should we make first? Who should speak first? Who will raise particular points or present particular pieces of information? Who will keep notes? Who will have the primary responsibility for trying to develop closure to the discussion? How long should we negotiate? How far can we compromise? How many points should we try for in a single negotiation effort?

- *Beware of cooptation.* Hardly a negotiation session occurs without someone's suggesting that a task force be formed to look into the matter. This is just one of many ways that negotiations can get sidetracked, defused, and forgotten. The negotiation session is already a task force. The negotiation session is the place where decisions need to be made. If additional time is needed for gathering more evidence or identifying possible solutions to a problem, then be sure to call for deadlines to ensure that the negotiations lead to conclusion.

- *Practice what we preach.* In order to convince others, it helps to have examples of what we mean right at hand. If we want schools to integrate severely disabled students into the mainstream of school life, for example, it helps to be able to say that we are doing our part to integrate our sons and daughters with disabilities in family life and in other aspects of community life.

- *Challenge excuses.* We have all heard the standard reasons why something cannot be done: "I'm sorry, but I am not in a position to make the decision." "The union would never go for it." "We have more than just your child to consider." "I'm sorry, but we just do not have the money." "You will have to be more patient." "Don't you think you are being a little unrealistic?" "You're too emotional." "We'll have to look into this." "We agree with you in philosophy, but we have to be practical." "We have much more information at our disposal than you could possibly have; therefore we are in a better position to make these kinds of decisions." "If we do this for you, we will have to do it for everyone." "It's against our policies." "That would jeopardize our insurance." "We like what you are suggesting, but you will have to give us more time." Parents can prepare responses to each of these excuses before negotiations ever begin.
- *Followup.* When will implementation occur? Who will be responsible? How long will it take? How will we measure success or failure? The terms of negotiation agreements should include each of these items.
- *Publicize negotiations.* Rarely should we regard negotiations as an activity that occurs behind closed doors. In most cases parents negotiate for more than one child. They are negotiating for new programs or changes in existing ones. Thus, many other families will be interested in, and affected by, the negotiations. We should report on the negotiations to other parents through press releases, newsletters, parent discussion groups, and special announcements.

BASIC RIGHTS

Every recent study of parents and their participation in promoting quality, integrated education programs, including the two studies upon which this book is based, confirms the importance of parents' being informed about their basic rights. As Brightman and Sullivan (1980) found, parents regard educational rights as their silent partner in advocacy. The following is a brief summary of the basic educational rights:

- The right to a free appropriate public education
- The right of parents to participate in the development of their child's individual education program
- The right to be informed about and to exercise due-process rights
- The right of parents to question a school's decision about how to classify, place, and serve their child
- The right to stop a change in classification or placement until after formally appealing the decision
- The right to see and make a copy of the child's complete school record
- The right to have the individual education program include information about the child's present performance, annual goals, short-term objectives, special and related services; to specify the extent of integration, dates and duration of programs, and the procedures for evaluating progress in programs
- The right to have all services mentioned in the IEP provided
- The right to education in the "least restrictive environment."

The federal law, Public Law 94–142 (1975), says that

> To the maximum extent appropriate, handicapped children, including children in public or private institutions or other care facilities, are educated with children who are not handicapped, . . .
> And that special classes, separate schooling or other removal of handicapped children from the regular educational environment occurs only when the nature or severity of the handicap is such that education in regular classes with the use of supplementary aids and services cannot be achieved satisfactorily.
> In providing or arranging for the provision of nonacademic and extracurricular services and activities, including meals, recess periods, and the services and activities set forth in section . . . [health services, transportation, athletics, counseling, special interest groups, clubs, etc.] each public agency shall insure that each handicapped child participates with non-handicapped children in those services and activities to the maximum extent appropriate to the needs of that child.

CONCLUSION

This chapter covers a broad range of situations, experiences and strategies. We have described situations in which schools and parents work hand in hand to achieve commonly held goals. And we have described nearly the opposite, where the relationship of parents to schools is estranged and where parents choose to rely on formal negotiating strategies to effect change. Obviously, most school administrators and teachers as well as most parents would prefer a positive relationship. The question is, How can that be accomplished?

We began the chapter with a premise that has surfaced throughout this book: that the parent perspective is not always, or even often, the same as that of a teacher or administrator. From our observations, we conclude that good school/parent relations develop when the parent perspective is not ignored or glossed over, but rather when it is recognized and considered. As one parent, Loyola Quinn, stated, "Schools and students miss out when parents are left out."

We found that parents of students with disabilities want essentially the same kinds of things from schools that parents of nondisabled students expect. These include access to education; continuity in the location of school programs so that the children, parents, and school staff can come to know each other over the years; the right to participate in parent/teacher organizations and activities; open dialogue with school officials on educational issues; and a spirit of cooperation. On the other hand, some of what parents want has specifically to do with the fact that their children have disabilities. They want their children to be free from a constant barrage of stereotyping. They want special education regarded as a regular part of the school program and not as an "experimental program" or as an "add on" or as a special tax burden. And they want school officials and teachers to take responsibility for learning about disabilities, about effective strategies for meeting the needs of disabled students, and about integration.

Increasingly, parents have relied on parent groups for various kinds of support. Many of these parent groups seem to have gotten their start when parents organized to improve school programs for disabled students. Some parent groups have provided personal support. Others have provided information and skills to parents on how to be a better parent. Others have had an advocacy orientation.

While we have not tried to mask the reality that parents and schools do not always interact harmoniously, we have observed and reported on numerous instances in which parent involvement is working. From these experiences and cases we have identified practical strategies that schools can use to foster parent involvement. These include such practices as: teacher interviews of parents about their children's strengths, weaknesses, and needs; involvement of parents in planning committees; combined parent/school efforts at community education about disabilities and integration programs; and making available self-help, parent-training, and special education materials to parents. Many of the exemplary integration programs began through parents' insistence and advocacy and later developed through a process of cooperation that emerged slowly, when parents and educators found effective ways of working together and of learning from each other.

6

Integration in School and Society

DOUGLAS BIKLEN

SPECIAL EDUCATION AT A CROSSROADS

Special education is at a crossroads. When special education was first recognized as a national problem in the late 1960s and early 1970s, the primary issues for students with disabilities were (1) whether or not they would achieve the right to an education; (2) if received, whether it would be a quality education; and (3) where that education would take place (i.e., in regular public schools, in private special schools, in segregated public schools, in institutions). While the issue of access is still with us—for example, many students who live in state institutions, who are wards of the state, who are poor, or who live in rural areas, still do not receive an education comparable to that received by other students—the primary issue of contention in special education is whether students will receive a quality education *in regular public schools*. In the previous chapters, we have focused almost no attention on the overall social context in which integration will rise or fall. Here we see as much need for change as in schools. It is quite clear that if the status of special education is to change and if integration has any chance at all of flourishing, the very basis of how we in this society think about disabilities must change, and change dramatically. Below we explore five principles that could help shape fuller integration for disabled students both in schools and in society.

FIVE PRINCIPLES: THE DIMENSIONS OF CHANGE

Principle 1: Equity requires an institutional commitment.

As long as we view integration as an experiment, we make its implementation tenuous. Equity for people with disabilities means no longer seeing accommodation (e.g., changes in architecture, provision of translators for people who sign) as something special or experimental but as something normal, as something that is institutionally guaranteed. In terms of schooling, this means that integration will proceed more easily where school districts and state departments of education have articulated a policy of integration, where they have initiated a formal planning process to guarantee integration, and where equity (e.g., in the form of integration) is not viewed as something that must be evaluated and judged effective before we can be committed to it.

That integration has not enjoyed broad-based institutional support is obvious. We live in a society where disability is still synonymous with different, marginal, or special. People with disabilities are not regularly considered as part of the populace. People with disabilities seldom appear in advertisements, except for special products. People with disabilities appear in literature and other popular media, but usually in stereotypes that emphasize the disabilities for some dramatic purpose. Similarly, most social policies that affect people with disabilities, even those intended to redress inequities, treat people with disabilities as special populations to be approached differently. Listen to the words of disability rights activists on such special treatment:

> Few people think about equality when they think about special.
>
> Assigning disabled people to special programs, giving them special buses and special schools, puts the community of disabled people in a ghetto. When the choice is between using the special service or doing without entirely, you really have no choice left.
>
> When blacks had no choices about where to live—but could live in only one area of town—that was called a ghetto.
>
> The lack of choice for integrated options for disabled people for transportation, for seating in places of public accommodation, for schooling; the provision of a special entrance, or a ramp at the back door or at the loading dock, of a "special elevator for the handicapped only," a "special restroom," are all signals that our society places disabled people in a ghetto too. ("What They Mean Is Segregated," 1983, p. 4)

Until accommodation for disabled is seen as regular, normal, and expected, it will be seen instead as special. As long as it is special, it will be, by definition, unequal. When we no longer need the term *special,* we will have achieved equality. A commitment to equity on an institutional level, in schools, in industry, in banks, in stores, in transportation and recreation, in social gathering places, and throughout society will go a long way toward making equality in our daily lives more winnable.

Principle 2: Activism, rights, and equity, not pity,
compassion, and benevolence, will foster the emergence
of integration.

Pity, compassion, benevolence, those are the banal companions of disability. Activism, rights, equity, those are the new images that people with disabilities and their allies seek. The language of Section 504 of the Rehabilitation Act captures this new spirit: "no otherwise qualified handicapped individual . . . shall, solely by reason of his handicap, be excluded from the participation in, be denied the benefits of, or be subjected to discrimination under any program or activity receiving federal financial assistance." But just as this antidiscrimination law heralded rights, so too did it symbolize the fact that people with disabilities rejected the notion that they were "charity cases."

As long as people with disabilities have had to depend on society's benevolence, rather than its respect, they have, to quote one disability rights activist, "gotten what we ask for, charity." Sally Johnston, another disability rights advocate, complains that charities portray people with disabilities alternatively as sad, tragic, and dependent, or cute, lovable, and pitiable. "Worst of all," she notes, "charities divert public attention from the real problems of having disabilities, the stereotyping, prejudice, and discrimination which people with disabilities are forced to endure day in and day out, year after year" (Biklen, et al., 1983).

Ironically, while most people think of benevolence, pity, and charitable giving as helpful, people with disabilities experience such treatment as debilitating, as part of the problem. Big-time charity campaigns epitomize the dilemma. Programs that serve people with disabilities often need contributions to survive, yet the most successful fund-raising techniques merely capitalize on and exacerbate the image of people with disabilities as poor, pitiable, and dependent. Many of the promotional materials picture sad, needy children; others make their appeal with children's smiles. Most charities resort to elaborate events such as telethons and circuses; even in these, however, they parade disabled children as if to say "Here are the poor souls your dollars will help." Devices that have traditionally been viewed by people with disabilities as liberating are portrayed as their enemy, more evidence that the nondisabled world has much to learn about disabilities. One such advertisement portrays a smiling child in an oversized wheelchair and challenges potential donors with the slogan "Be a miracle worker," as if to say her chief problem in life is her need to use a wheelchair. Similarly, another fund appeal called on donors to pitch dollars and change into a glass box with a brace inside. The slogan read, "Help Jerry's kids bury the brace." ("Jerry" refers to entertainer Jerry Lewis, who chairs the Muscular Dystrophy Association annual telethon.)

To some extent, we still see the charity mentality in schools. Every time a school official complains of the costs of special education or considers those costs only after the balance of school programs have been attended to, we bear witness to the fact that special education is perceived as an "add on," something that will be given, as if an act of charity, after the "regular" programs. Just as schools must continue to struggle against the charity mentality, so too must society at large. It is time we reclaim the true meaning of charity, to show good will *and* high regard for all people.

Principle 3: Normalization must become part of everyday life.

The concept of normalization has been central to integrating students with disabilities in regular public schools. It is a guiding principle. Simply stated, it means, "Treat people with disabilities as normally as possible." In the world of education it means using teaching strategies that are as typical as possible. Yet it is obvious that schools cannot effectively promote normalization without broad-based support for the concept throughout society. What is the point, for example, of creating a school world devoid of such things as name calling, stereotyping, forced congregation of people on the basis of their disabilities, or condescending pity, if they must enter and live in a larger world that encourages these same behaviors?

In his now classic book, *Of Mice and Men*, John Steinbeck portrays social struggle rife with handicapist stereotypes. In fact it is fair to say that the book itself promotes handicapism, the opposite of normalization. The story centers around two hired hands, Lenny and George. Lenny is the stereotypical he-man, a big, dumb, bumbling man, with a heart of gold, who does not know his own strength. George, the smarter of the two, is portrayed as smaller and more clever. We are asked to believe that their physical appearance in some way explains their characters:

> They had walked in single file down the path, and even in the open one stayed behind the other. Both were dressed in denim trousers and in denim coats with brass buttons. Both wore black, shapeless hats and both carried tight blanket rolls slung over their shoulders. The first man was small and quick, dark of face, with restless eyes and sharp, strong features. Every part of him was defined: small, strong hands, slender arms, a thin and bony nose. Behind him walked his opposite, a huge man, shapeless of face, with large, pale eyes, with wide, sloping shoulders; and he walked heavily, dragging his feet a little, the way a bear drags his paws. His arms did not swing at his sides, but hung loosely. (Steinbeck, 1955, p. 2)

Throughout the book, Lenny is portrayed as the hapless King Kong type of character who is incompetent and dangerous, but also warm, kind-hearted, and likeable. Only George seems to understand him, though even he exploits Lenny and subtly demeans him. In the end, after Lenny has accidentally killed a puppy and a flirtatious woman, and just when a group of angry pursuers are about to catch him and surely do him in, George shoots Lenny in the back of the neck, as if to save him from facing death at the hands of a small mob. All of this leaves the reader with a feeling not only of sadness, but of hopelessness as well. The disabled person was so problematic, so incompetent, if kind, so strong and yet also so uncontrolled, that his only salvation is his own death. He was a person who was miserably taunted. Even the person who cared for him most, George, seldom treated him as a normal person. We are shown no truly normalizing attitudes or treatment toward Lenny nor, for that matter, how he might have responded.

It is these types of stereotypes that we must challenge. Society must find ways of promoting normalization in everyday situations if the advances of normalization in schools are to have any chance of proliferating in the society at large. In schools we see students being grouped in natural proportion; we see teachers changing their ways of referring to students, shunning unnecessary labeling; we see teachers interacting with disabled students in ways similar to how they relate to nondisabled students. How can we identify similar strategies for promoting normalization in society at large?

Actually, there is a simple method of developing normalization strategies for the community. These would have worked well for the people who knew Lenny. They can work well for us. All we need to do is ask ourselves the question, "How would I like to be treated?" In answering that question in a broad range of social situations, we will hit on many effective strategies for promoting normalization.

Harper Lee, in the book *To Kill a Mockingbird*, offers us a glimpse of normalization in practice. This book possessed all of the same opportunities for stereotyping that were present in Steinbeck's *Of Mice and Men*. But Lee proffers a different view. Near the conclusion to the novel, two children, Jem and Jean Louise, are attacked in the woods. Shortly thereafter, Jean Louise is asked by her father (Atticus) and the sheriff to identify the person who saved her brother and herself from greater harm. It turns out that the good Samaritan is none other than Arthur Radley, known to the children as Boo, a retarded man who seems to live as a "shut-in" next door to where the children and their father live. We pick up the dialogue at the point where Jean Louise identifies Mr. Radley as the person who saved her brother and herself:

> "Why there he is, Mr. Tate, he can tell you his name." As I said it, I half pointed to the man in the corner, but brought my arm down quickly lest Atticus reprimand me for pointing. It was impolite to point. . . .
>
> When I pointed to him his palms slipped slightly, leaving greasy sweat streaks on the wall, and he hooked his thumbs in his belt. A strange small spasm shook him, as if he heard fingernails scrape slate, but as I gazed at him in wonder the tension slowly drained from his face. His lips parted into a timid smile, and our neighbor's image blurred with my sudden tears.
>
> "Hey, Boo," I said.
>
> "Mr. Arthur, honey," said Atticus, gently correcting me.
>
> "Jean Louise, this is Mr. Arthur Radley. I believe he already knows you."
>
> If Atticus could blandly introduce me to Boo Radley at a time like this, well—that was Atticus.
>
> Boo saw me run instinctively to the bed where Jem was sleeping, for the same shy smile crept across his face. (Lee, 1960, p. 273)

> "Will you take me home?"
>
> He almost whispered it, in the voice of a child afraid of the dark.
>
> I put my foot on the top step and stopped. I would lead him through our house, but I would never lead him home.

"Mr. Arthur, bend your arm down here, like that. That's right, sir."

I slipped my hand into the crook of his arm. He had to stoop a little to accommodate me, but if Miss Stephanie Crawford was watching from her upstairs window [a woman in the neighborhood who told wild tales about Mr. Radley], she would see Arthur Radley escorting me down the sidewalk, as any gentleman would do. (Lee, 1960, p. 281)

Notice the author Harper Lee's attention to what we now call normalization. She has Atticus correct Jean Louise for pointing at Mr. Radley and for calling him Boo. Then she shows Jean Louise walking with Mr. Radley. In each instance we were presented with a situation in which Mr. Radley could have been stereotyped as an incompetent person, perhaps as a child or, as in the case of Lenny, as almost animallike. Yet Lee selects a different image. Arthur Radley is treated as a peer, as someone who is capable of understanding, of helping, of dignity.

The image that Harper Lee fashions is one that schools have begun to demonstrate as well, namely treating people with disabilities in nonstereotyped ways. As we have seen, some schools have gone about this in a structured way. They have identified concepts and practices that support the goal of normalization and have introduced these into schools systematically. In this sense, schools have modeled ideas and practices that society could use on a wider scale. These strategies include, for example: learning from people with disabilities about their lives, their experiences, and their aspirations; minimizing exceptionalistic language that sets individuals and groups apart as different; using natural strategies of education as much as possible with people who have disabilities; believing and stating that concern for people with disabilities and with such matters as accessibility and other forms of accommodation are everyone's responsibility, not simply that of the special education profession; rejecting automatic and unnecessary segregation; assuming an attitude of problem solving; identifying opportunities and barriers that people with disabilities will face and preparing people with disabilities to confront these; abandoning the idea that a disability is all-defining of a person and, instead, recognizing it as but one quality among many; believing in the educability and development of every person; recording change and garnering optimism from it; rejecting a medical orientation to people with disabilities; and recognizing that the greatest difficulties faced by people with disabilities are not the disabilities themselves but are rather the stereotyping, prejudice, and discrimination that they experience because they have disabilities.

If there were no discrimination against people with disabilities, if there were no stereotyping and prejudice, there would be no need for words like "normalization," "mainstreaming," and "integration." But we are far from that point. We still have transportation systems set up to serve the nondisabled. We still see no people with disabilities in commercial advertisements except for disability-related products. Job discrimination is rampant; two-thirds of all people with disabilities are unemployed.

It is time for us to learn from the experience of schools. In schools we have seen practical and effective integration strategies. In many instances schools themselves have initiated change outside of schools, for example through non-school-based vocational and domestic training. We now need a concerted program of change in society. The disability rights movement has of course done much already in terms of community organizing, protesting demeaning charity campaigns, demanding accessibility, criticizing human abuse in nursing homes and other institutions, and demanding an antidiscrimination law. But the problem of people with disabilities does not belong to "the disabled" or to the professions that provide services to people with disabilities. It belongs to us all. It is our collective duty to view people with disabilities as the competent, feeling, multifaceted people they are. It is for all of us to refrain from stereotyping people with disabilities as pitiable, sad, or adorable. We can all work to guarantee the fullest possible integration of disabled and nondisabled people in society. We can all work to ensure public, universally available basic services (for example, education, health care, transportation) so that people with disabilities will no longer need to beg for them.

Principle 4: Working with people who have disabilities is important.

It is often said that the status of a profession correlates directly with the perceived status of its clientele and the degree to which the ideas and practices of the profession are thought to be esoteric. If this is the case, special education will most likely not rank as a high-status profession. First, its clientele are perpetually the objects of stereotyping, prejudice, and discrimination. In most quarters they hold low status. True, there is nothing in the natural order that says people with disabilities must be the objects of such a fate; after all, stereotyping, prejudice, and discrimination are socially created. Yet, as we have seen so often in this culture, people with disabilities have not always enjoyed equality or even respect. Second, special education, like much of education in general, particularly elementary education, has been perceived as only slightly more sophisticated than babysitting. And since most people can easily understand the material used in special and elementary curricula, the profession of special education may not seem so special and certainly not esoteric. Compared to law, to most aspects of medicine, even to high school education, special education appears on the surface at least to be relatively unsophisticated. To the extent that special education has incorporated medical terminology and presented curricular strategies in technical terms, it has gained more special status.

As we have noted earlier, we can perceive special education's low status in such commonly heard statements as the following:

Can these people really benefit from an education?
How much can society afford to spend on this; we don't have unlimited resources you know.
Isn't it terribly frustrating work when you don't see progress?
Isn't it mainly babysitting?
I like working with bright kids, but I'd get depressed if I had to work with the handicapped.

And so it goes. Each statement presents the problem of negative attitudes toward people with disabilities. To call special education babysitting is to deny its educational value and to render children and youth with disabilities babies or, at least, babylike. To call education of people with disabilities sad is to judge people with disabilities and their lives as pathetic. To raise the matter of expense in providing special education is to suggest that it is added on to regular education, something that should be considered as a separate enterprise. To speak of special education as inherently frustrating is to fail to understand the possible creativity in it. And to imply that people with disabilities might not profit from educational programming in much the same way that other people benefit from it is to consign people with disabilities to a state of ensured or enforced incompetence.

The status of special education will probably not improve until either society recognizes and/or the profession of special education articulates the creative challenge and rewards inherent in special education. Teaching a student with a severe physical disability to communicate can, admittedly, prove difficult. How can a student with severe cerebral palsy voice sounds into words? For some this is tortuous. But the problem is one that the profession of special education can find challenging. Recently, educators are turning to computers, sign language, communication boards, voice synthesizers, and other technologies to facilitate students' communication.

How can teachers best help students moving from an institution to the community learn to act in ways that are appropriate for community living? How can teachers help them shed the institutional behaviors such as foot shuffling, excessive and inappropriate hugging, rocking, talking out loud when not engaged in conversation, and attitudes of defeatism? How can teachers help them learn basic community living skills, and the like? As we have noted in several earlier chapters, many schools have developed programs to perform just these tasks, to answer just these questions. For these schools and their teachers, special education has been an exciting field, filled with complex challenges.

To confront such challenges is to engage in detective work. We must constantly ask, "What method will work?" Or, "Have we discovered the method that can work?" As we noted in our chapter on teachers, it was not too long ago that most educators regarded the "developmental model" of education as the most viable approach to sequencing special education curricula. But some educators, faced with repeated difficulties in getting their students past certain developmental levels—indeed, for these teachers, levels were more like immutable hurdles—began to ask, "Is there another model?" Eventually they adopted what has come to be called the functional model. With this approach, rather than assuming that a student had to progress in a more or less orderly and predictable sequence from one level to the next before acquiring the skills to assimilate other skills, behavior, or knowledge, curricula could focus on the subject content most related to students' needs to become independent in the community.

As each of these examples suggests, special education has not remained, if it ever was, a stagnant, pathetic, boring, unchallenging, unintellectual enterprise. Now we must communicate that to society at large.

Principle 5: The success of integration throughout society will be determined by our commitment to it.

In the first chapter we discussed briefly the controversy over integration. Some people would have us wait for science, in this case educational researchers, to prove that integration yields faster, more effective learning than does segregation. But, as we have suggested, to look to science for an answer to the question, "Is integration a good idea?" is like asking, "Is religion a good idea?" or "Is it good and right for people to care for their aging parents?" In other words, the practice of integrating disabled people with the nondisabled is not fundamentally a question that science can answer. From science we can learn some of the effects of such a policy (e.g., in terms of learning rates, types of education possible, nature of interaction between disabled and nondisabled), or how to make it work better, but science cannot tell us that integration is right. In fact, we have much evidence from painstaking observations and careful recording to suggest obvious benefits from integration, but we know that this question of whether to integrate or not is really an ethical question. We can answer it only by determining what we believe, what we consider important.

Ethics is the study and practice of moral behavior. Whether to integrate is a moral concern, not a factual one. We can call upon facts to help inform us and perhaps to influence ethical decisions, but facts cannot replace moral judgment. Whether to integrate is every bit as much an ethical concern as is the decision of whether to provide free medical treatment to people who cannot pay for it themselves or whether to provide college education to bright high school graduates.

In the case of integration, in schools and throughout society, we may witness competing value issues. Belief in one value may, in a real-life situation, conflict with another. Assume, for example, that we can agree on the following values:

1. Integrated education for disabled and nondisabled students
2. Promoting outstanding academic performance by students with exceptional intelligence

In a practical situation, it is quite possible that in the interest of value 2 we would want to provide special research-laboratory programs or computer-theory courses to young, bright students. We might judge it inappropriate to provide these same experiences to certain disabled students, for example, to students with autism or mental retardation. To further complicate matters, we might want to provide severely disabled students basic self-help living skills. Such programming would be unnecessary for the students for whom we designed computer-theory courses. But, in implementing these various programs, each in the interest of promoting value 2, we seem to have created a conflict with value 1, our desire to promote integration. In pursuing 2 we have driven some disabled students away from some nondisabled students.

Does this mean that we have abandoned value 1? No, not at all. We may still believe in value 1 but we may be faced with a dilemma: Under these conditions, how can we implement it? We can perhaps find other areas of programming where integration can occur, in the lunchroom, in social and recreational settings, in homeroom, in school performances, and on school busses. We can locate classes of students with severe disabilities near students with no disabilities. The point is that even though we must give one value priority over another in certain situations, we do not have to abandon the lesser value. In this case, if we believe in integration we can use our creativity to discover ways of promoting it, even when other values intrude upon us.

We began this chapter by warning of a crisis in special education. This crisis is no different from the challenge faced by any social change movement. After the initial enthusiasm, confrontation, experimentation, and success, the newness wears off. Some of what was promised fails to materialize. Some change efforts backfire. Some may even prove harmful. Hence the concern, the sense of crisis. Yet despite the predictable state we are in, we find reason for optimism. As the experiences of schools and teachers suggest, at least those we observed and report on here, we are finding practical, creative ways of making integration work. These experiences, this evidence, bear witness to the fact that if we can extricate ourselves from the false notions that science rather than ethics will tell us whether to integrate, or that different values cannot coexist, and instead embrace integration as a matter of ethics and as something practical and possible, then we can get on with the creative, complex, rewarding task of finding strategies and approaches to make it work even better. For this, experimentation and research, the tools of science, can be most helpful.

To summarize, success with integration in schools depends on and also fuels integration in society at large. Five principles facilitate the social transformation:

- Equity requires an institutional commitment.
- Activism, rights, and equity, not pity, compassion, and benevolence, will foster the emergence of integration.

- Normalization can be a part of everyday life.
- Working with people who have disabilities is important.
- The success of integration will be determined by our commitment to it.

REFERENCES

ABOUT THE AUTHORS

INDEX

References

Apolloni, T., Cooke, S. A., and Cooke, T. P. Establishing a normal peer as a behavioral model for developmentally delayed children. *Perceptual and Motor Skills,* 1977, *44*, 231–241.

Apolloni, T., Cooke, T. P. Integrated programming at the infant, toddler, and preschool age levels. In M. J. Guralnick (Ed.), *Early intervention and the integration of handicapped and non-handicapped children.* Baltimore, MD: University Park Press, 1978.

Arkell, C. J., Thomason, J., and Haring, N. Deinstitutionalization of a residential facility. *The Journal of the Association of the Severely Handicapped,* 1980, *5*, 107–120.

Audette, R. Interagency collaboration: The bottom line. In J. O. Elder and P. R. Magrab, *Coordinating services to handicapped children: A handbook for interagency collaboration.* Baltimore, MD: Paul Brookes Publishers, 1980.

Barnes, E. *Peer relationships between typical and severely disturbed children in an integrated setting.* Unpublished doctoral dissertation, Syracuse University, 1978.

Barnes, E., Berrigan, C., and Biklen, D. *What's the difference: Teaching positive attitudes toward people with disabilities.* Syracuse, NY: Human Policy Press, 1978.

Biklen, D., and Bailey, L. *Rudely stamp'd.* Washington, DC: University Press of America, 1979.

Biklen, D., and Bogdan, R. *Handicapism* [Slideshow]. Syracuse, NY: Human Policy Press, 1976.

Biklen, D., Bogdan, R., Shapiro, A., Spelkoman, D. *The charity case* [Slideshow]. Syracuse, NY: Human Policy Press, 1983.

Biklen, D., and Sokoloff, M. *What do you do when your wheelchair gets a flat tire?* New York: Scholastic Magazine, Inc., 1978.

Blatt, B. *Exodus from pandemonium.* Boston: Allyn and Bacon, 1969.

Blatt, B., Bogdan, R., Biklen, D., and Taylor, S. From institution to community: A conversion model. In E. Sontag, J. Smith, and N. Certo (Eds.), *Educational programming for the severely and profoundly handicapped.* Reston, VA: Council for Exceptional Children, 1977.

Blatt, B., McNally, J., and Ozolins, A. *The family papers.* New York: Longmans, 1980.

Bogdan, R. "Does mainstreaming work?" is a silly question. *Phi Delta Kappan,* 1983, *64,* 427–428.

Bogdan, R., Taylor, S., deGrandpre, B., and Haynes, S. Let them eat programs: Attendants' perspectives and programming on wards in state schools. *Journal of Health and Social Behavior,* 1974, *15*(2), 142–150.

Bookbinder, S. R. *Meeting street school curriculum*. Boston, MA: Exceptional Parent Press, 1978.

Bricker, D. D. A rationale for the integration of handicapped and nonhandicapped school children. In M. J. Guralnick (Ed.), *Early intervention and the integration of handicapped and nonhandicapped children*. Baltimore, MD: University Park Press, 1978.

Brightman, A. "But their brain is broken": Young children's conceptions of retardation. In M. Harmonay (Ed.), *Promise and performance: ACT's guide to T.V. programming for children*. Children with Special Needs. Cambridge, MA: Ballinger Books, 1977.

Brightman, A., and Sullivan, M. *The impact of Public Law 94–142 on parents of disabled children: A report of findings*. Cambridge, MA: The Cambridge Workshop, Inc., 37 Goden St., Belmont, MA 02146, October 15, 1980.

Brown, L., Branston, M. B., Baumgart, D., Vincent, L., Falvey, M., and Schroeder, J. Utilizing the characteristics of a variety of current and subsequent least restrictive environments as factors in the development of curricular content for severely handicapped students. In L. Brown, M. Falvey, D. Baumgart, I. Pumpian, J. Schroeder, and L. Gruenewald (Eds.), *Strategies for teaching chronological age appropriate functional skills to adolescent and young adult severely handicapped students* (Vol. 9, Part 1). Madison, WI: Madison Metropolitan School District, 1979a. Revised and republished: *Journal of Special Education*, 1980, *14*(2), 199–215.

Brown, L., Branston, M. B., Hamre-Nietupski, S., Johnson, F., Wilcox, B., and Gruenewald, L. A rationale for comprehensive longitudinal interactions between severely handicapped students and nonhandicapped students and other citizens. *AAESPH Review*, 1979b, *4*(1), 3–14.

Brown, L., Branston, M. B., Hamre-Nietupski, S., Pumpian, I., Certo, N., and Gruenewald, L. A strategy for developing chronological age appropriate and functional curricular content for severely handicapped adolescents and young adults. *Journal of Special Education*, 1979c, *13* (1), 81–90.

Brown, L., Falvey, M., Vincent, L., Kaye, N., Johnson, F., Ferrara-Parrish, P., and Gruenewald, L. Strategies for generating comprehensive, longitudinal and chronological age appropriate individual educational plans for adolescent and young adult severely handicapped students. In L. Brown, M. Falvey, D. Baumgart, I. Pumpian, J. Schroeder, and L. Gruenewald (Eds.), *Strategies for teaching chronological age appropriate functional skills to adolescent and young adult severely handicapped students* (Vol. 9, Part 1). Madison, WI: Madison Metropolitan School District, 1979d.

Brown, L., Pumpian, I., Baumgart, D., Van Deventer, P., Ford, A., Nisbet, J., Schroeder, J., and Gruenewald, L. Longitudinal transition plans in programs for severely handicapped students. *Exceptional Children*, 1981, *47*, 624–631.

Brown, L., Wilcox, B., Sontag, E., Vincent, B., Dodd, N., and Gruenewald, L. Toward the realization of the least restrictive educational environment for severely handicapped students. In L. Brown, J. Nietupski, S. Lyon, S. Hamre-Nietupski, T. Crowner, and L. Gruenewald (Eds.), *Curricular strategies for teaching functional object use, nonverbal communication, problem solving, and mealtime skills to severely handicapped students* (Vol. 3, Part 1). Madison, WI: Madison

Metropolitan School District, 1977, 1–13. [Also published *AAESPH Review,* 1977, 2, 195–201.]

Burrello, L. C., and Sage, D. *Leadership and change in special education.* Englewood Cliffs, NJ: Prentice-Hall, 1979.

Children's Defense Fund. *Children out of school in America.* Washington, DC: Children's Defense Fund, 1974.

Cohen, S. *Accepting individual differences.* Niles, IL: Developmental Learning Materials, 1977.

Cruickshank, W. M. Least-restrictive placement: administrative wishful thinking. *Journal of Learning Disabilities,* 1977, *10,* 193–194.

Cutler, B. C. *Unraveling the special education maze.* Champaign, IL: Research Press, 1981.

Davies, S. P. The institution in relation to the school system. In M. Rosen, G. R. Clark, and M. Kinitz (Eds.), *The history of mental retardation.* Baltimore, MD: University Park Press, 1976.

Davis, E. D. *Promising practices in mainstreaming for the secondary school principal.* (ERIC, EC112317, 17 pp.). Washington, DC: National Institute of Education, 1977.

Deno, E. Special education or developmental capital. *Exceptional Children,* November 1970, 229–237.

Donahue, P. *My own story.* New York: Simon and Schuster, 1979.

Dybwad, G. Avoiding misconceptions of mainstreaming, the least restrictive environment, and normalization. *Exceptional Children,* 1980, *47,* 85–88.

Dunn, Lloyd M. "Special education for the mildly retarded—Is much of it justifiable?" *Exceptional Children,* 1968, *35,* 5–22.

Eaton, J. W., and Weil, R. J. *Culture and mental disorders: A comparative study of Hutterites and other populations.* Glencoe, IL: Free Press, 1955.

Gage, K. H. The principal's role in implementing mainstreaming. *Educational Leadership,* 1979, *36,* 575–577.

Georgia Learning Resources System & National Association of State Directors of Special Education, Inc. *Questions and answers on surrogate parents: A resource guide for special education administrators.* Atlanta, GA: Metro-West Georgia Learning Resources Center, 1980.

Gilhool, T., and Stutman, E. Integration of severely handicapped students toward criteria for implementing and enforcing the integration imperative of P.L. 94–142 and section 504. In *Criteria for the evaluation of the least restrictive environment provision.* Washington, DC: Bureau of Education for the Handicapped, Department of Health, Education and Welfare, 1978.

Goffman, E. *Stigma.* Englewood Cliffs, NJ: Prentice-Hall, 1963.

Goldstein, H., Moss, J. W., and Jordon, L. *The efficacy of special class training of the development of mentally retarded children* (U.S.O.E., Cooperative Research Report No. 619). Urbana: University of Illinois, 1965.

Goodlad, J. *A place called school.* New York: McGraw-Hill, 1984.

Gottlieb, J. Attitudes toward retarded children: Effects of labeling and academic performance. *American Journal of Mental Deficiency,* 1974, *79,* 268–273.

Gottlieb, J. Placement in the least restrictive environment. In *Criteria for the evaluation of the least restrictive environment provision.* Washington, D.C: Bureau of Education for the Handicapped, Department of Health, Education and Welfare, 1978.

Greenberg, J., and Doolittle, G. Can schools speak the language of the deaf? *The New York Times Magazine,* Dec. 11, 1977, pp. 50ff.

Grund, W. *A comparative study of factors associated with programming practices for handicapped children in school districts using local versus cooperative service delivery.* Unpublished doctoral dissertation, Syracuse University, 1976.

Guralnick, M. J. Social interactions among preschool children. *Exceptional Children,* 1980, *46,* 248–253.

Guralnick, M. J. (Ed.). *Early intervention and the integration of handicapped and non-handicapped children.* Baltimore, MD: University Park Press, 1978.

Hale, G. *The sourcebook for the disabled.* New York: Paddington Press, 1979.

Hambleton, D., and Ziegler, S. *The study of the integration of trainable retarded students into a regular elementary school setting.* Toronto: Metropolitan Toronto School Board, Research Department, 1974.

Herbel, W. A study of the costs incurred by Kansas local education agencies in the provision of special education service. *Dissertation Abstracts International, 38.* (University Microfilms, 1977, No. 77–16, 326, 160 pp.).

Kleinfeld, S. *The hidden minority.* Boston: Little Brown, 1979.

Knoblock, P. *Teaching and mainstreaming autistic children.* Denver: Love Publishing, 1982.

Knoblock, P., and Barnes, E. Children learn together: A model program integrating severely disturbed children into an open setting. In S. Meisels (Ed.), *Open education and young children with special needs.* Baltimore, MD: University Park Press, 1979.

Kugel, R. B., and Wolfensberger, W. *Changing patterns in residential services for the mentally retarded.* Washington, DC: President's Committee on Mental Retardation, 1969.

Lee, H. *To kill a mockingbird.* New York: Popular Library, 1960.

Lippman, L., and Goldberg, I. *Right to education.* New York: Teachers College Press, 1973.

Loyola Quinn v. Niskayuna Central School District, 1979. (An appeal before the Commissioner of Education, New York State.)

McLaurin v. Oklahoma State Regents for Higher Education, 339 U.S. 637 (1950).

Mills v. the Board of Education of the District of Columbia, 348 F. Supp. 866 (D.D.C. 1972).

National Education Association. *Education for all handicapped children: Consensus, conflict and challenge, a study report.* Washington, DC: NEA, 1978.

Nietupski, J., Hamre-Nietupski, S., Schuetz, G., and Ockwood, L. *Severely handicapped students in regular schools: A progress report: Milwaukee Public Schools integration efforts.* Milwaukee: Milwaukee Public Schools, 1980.

Northcutt, W. *The hearing-impaired child in a regular classroom.* Washington, DC: Alexander Graham Bell Association for the Deaf, 1973.

NYSARC v. Carey, 466 F. Supp. 479 (E.D. N.Y. 1978) and 466 F. Supp. 487 (E.D. N.Y. 1979).

Paul, J., Turnbull, A., Cruickshank, W. *Mainstreaming: A practical guide.* Syracuse, NY: Syracuse University Press, 1977.

Pennsylvania Association for Retarded Children v. the Commonwealth of Pennsylvania, 334 F. Supp. 1257 (E.D. Pa. 1971).

Perske, R. *Mental retardation: The leading edge.* Washington, D.C.: President's Committee on Mental Retardation, 1979.

Pieper, E. *Sticks and stones.* Syracuse, NY: Human Policy Press, 1977.

Polloway, E. A., and Snell, M. E. Efficacy revisited. *Education and Training of the Mentally Retarded,* 1975, *10*(4), 277–282.

Public Law 94–142, the Right to Education for All Handicapped Children Act, 1975, 20 U.S.C. §1412.

Pumpian, I., Livi, J., Falvey, M., Loomis, R., and Brown, L. Strategies for generating curricular content to teach adolescent and young adult severely handicapped students domestic living skills. In L. Brown, M. Falvey, D. Baumgart, I. Pumpian, J. Schroeder, and L. Gruenewald (Eds.), *Strategies for teaching chronological age appropriate functional skills to adolescent and young adult severely handicapped students* (Vol. 9, Part 1). Madison, WI: Madison Metropolitan School District, 1979.

Rehabilitation Act of 1973, §504, 29 U.S.C. §701–796.

Reynolds, Maynard D. A framework for considering some issues in special education. *Exceptional Children,* 1962, *28*, 367–370.

Rice, R. G. *A cost-quality analysis of special education programs.* Unpublished doctoral dissertation. Syracuse University, 1975.

Ritchie, D. S., Gruenewald, L. J., and Schroeder, J. *Integration of moderately and severely handicapped students in public schools.* Paper presented at the Organization for Cooperation and Development, Paris, France, November 1979.

Robson, D. L. Administering educational services for the handicapped: Role expectations and perception. *Exceptional Children,* 1981, *47*, 377–378.

Sailor, W., and Haring, N. Progress in the education of the severely/profoundly handicapped. In N. Haring and D. Bricker (Eds.), *Teaching the severely handicapped* (Vol. 3). Seattle: AAESPH, 1978.

Sailor, W., Wilcox, B., and Brown, L. (Eds.). *Methods of instruction for severely handicapped students.* Baltimore, MD: Paul Brookes, 1980.

Sarason, S. The mismanagement model. *Social Policy,* September/October 1981, 51–52.

Sarason, S., and Doris, J. *Educational handicap, public policy and social history.* New York: Free Press, 1979.

Sarason, S. B., and Gladwin, T. *Psychological and cultural problems in mental subnormality: A review of research.* Provincetown, MA: Genetic Psychology Monographs, 1958.

Sarson, C., Brightman, A., and Blatt, J. *Feeling free* [Films]. New York: Scholastic Magazine, Inc., 1978.

Scheerenberger, R. C. *A history of mental retardation.* Baltimore, MD: Paul Brookes, 1983.

Scheerenberger, R. C. *Public residential services for the mentally retarded 1981.* Madison, WI: National Association of Superintendents of Public Residential Facilities for the Mentally Retarded, 1982.

Scholl, G. T. Visually handicapped children in the regular class. *Teacher,* February 1978, pp. 79–80.

Schopler, E., and Olley, J. G. Comprehensive educational services for autistic children: The TEACCH model. In T. B. Gutkin and C. R. Reynolds (Eds.), *A handbook for the practice of school psychology.* New York: John Wiley, in press.

Shanker, A. Help ahead for handicapped but . . . new law also creates some problems. *New York Times,* March 20, 1977, IV, 7:5.

Sousie, S., Edelman, S., Christie, L., Fox, T., Fox, W., Hill, M., William, W., and York, R. *Providing interdisciplinary support to teachers in rural settings.* Burlington, VT: Center for Developmental Disabilities, University of Vermont, 1978.

Special Education Resource Center. *Special populations: Compendium of practices.* Syracuse, NY: Special Education Resource Center, Syracuse University, 1982.

Steinbeck, J. *Of Mice and Men.* New York: Viking Press, 1955.

Stephens, T. M., Blackhurst, A. E., and Magliocca, L. A. *Teaching mainstreamed students.* New York: John Wiley, 1982.

Sternat, J., Messina, R., Nietupski, J., Lyon, S., and Brown, L. Occupational and physical therapy services for severely handicapped students: Toward a naturalized public school service delivery model. In E. Sontag, J. Smith, and N. Certo (Eds.), *Educational programming for the severely and profoundly handicapped.* Reston, VA: Council for Exceptional Children, 1977.

Stetson, F. E., Elting, S. E., Gibbs, L. K., Raimondi, S. L., Burnette, J., and Scheffter, A. *Options: A training program to present administrative options for implementing the least restrictive environment (LRE) mandate.* Annandale, VA: JWK International Corporation, 1981.

Sturlken, E. H. Some guiding principles: Segregation vs. nonsegregation. *Proceedings of the 22nd Annual Meeting, International Council for Exceptional Children,* 1946.

Task Force on Children Out of School. *The way we go to school.* Boston: Beacon Press, 1969.

Taylor, S. J. From segregation to integration: Strategies for integrating severely handicapped students in normal school and community settings. *Journal of the Association for the Severely Handicapped,* 1983, *8,* 42–49.

Taylor, S. J., and Bogdan, R. Defending illusions: The institution's struggle for survival. *Human Organization,* 1980, *39* (3), 209–218.

Thomas, K. *Rhode Island surrogate parent program: Parent resource manual.* Providence, RI: Rhode Island Department of Education, 1980.

Vermont Surrogate Parent Program. *Annual work plan.* Vermont: VSPP, n.d.

Vincent, L., and Broome, K. A public school service delivery model for handicapped children between birth and five years of age. In E. Sontag, J. Smith, and N. Certo (Eds.), *Educational programming for the severely and profoundly handicapped.* Reston, VA: Division of Mental Retardation, Council on Exceptional Children, 1977.

Vincent, L., Salisbury, C., Walter, G., Brown, P., Gruenewald, L., and Powers, M. Program evaluation and curriculum development in early childhood/special education: Criteria of the next environment. In W. Sailor, B. Wilcox, and L. Brown (Eds.), *Instructional design for the severely handicapped.* Baltimore, MD: Paul Brookes, 1980.

Voeltz, L. M. Children's attitudes toward handicapped peers. *American Journal of Mental Deficiency,* 1980, *85,* 268–283.

Voeltz, L. M. Effects of structured interactions with severely handicapped peers on children's attitudes. *American Journal of Mental Deficiency,* 1982, *86,* 180–190.

Waller, W. *The sociology of teaching.* New York: John Wiley, 1976 (1932).

What they mean is segregated. *The Disability Rag,* August 1983, 3–4.

Williams, W., and Fox, T. (Eds.). *Minimum objective system for pupils with severe handicaps.* Burlington, VT: Center for Developmental Disabilities, University of Vermont, 1977.

Wolfensberger, W. *The origin and nature of our institutional models.* Syracuse, NY: Human Policy Press, 1975.

Wolfensberger, W. *The principle of normalization in human services.* Toronto: National Institute on Mental Retardation, 1972.

Wolfensberger, W. Social role valorization: a proposed new term for the principle of normalization. *Mental Retardation,* 1983, *21,* 234–239.

Yuker, H. Attitudes or determinants of behavior, *Journal of Rehabilitation,* 1965, *31,* 15–16.

About the Authors

DOUGLAS BIKLEN is Professor and Director of the Division of Special Education and Rehabilitation at Syracuse University. His research areas of specialization are social policy and disability, integrated schooling, deinstitutionalization, and media treatment of disabilities. He has authored and coauthored books and articles on such topics as child advocacy, community organizing, law and special education, and attitude change. He earned his Ph.D. in social science at Syracuse University.

ROBERT BOGDAN is Professor of Special Education and of Sociology at Syracuse University. His professional work has been in qualitative research methods, ethnographies of people with mental retardation, and the sociology of disabilities. In his research he has examined such diverse programs as Headstart, deinstitutionalization, institutions for mentally retarded and mentally ill people, neonatal hospital units, and schools. His Ph.D. is in sociology from Syracuse University.

DIANNE L. FERGUSON is Assistant Professor of Special Education at the University of Oregon. Her areas of specialization are curriculum for severely disabled students, early education, and social policy and disability. She has worked as a program administrator in special education, as a teacher, and as a researcher. She is the parent of a child with a severe disability. She earned her Ph.D. in special education at Syracuse University.

STANFORD J. SEARL, JR. is Executive Director of East End Community Services, Inc., a non-profit home health care and family support service on eastern Long Island, New York. He is a former staff member of the Center on Human Policy at Syracuse University. He holds a Ph.D. in English and a master's degree in public administration, both from Syracuse

University. He served previously as an Associate Professor of English at the State University of New York College at Buffalo. His professional interests are in community-based alternatives to institutions, independent living, integrated education, and policy development and analysis. Also, he continues to work as a writer and editor in connection with American studies and Quaker history.

STEVEN J. TAYLOR is Director of the Center on Human Policy at Syracuse University. He has written extensively on models of integrated education for students with disabilities, independent living services, deinstitutionalization, national medicaid policy, and qualitative research. With Robert Bogdan, he has coauthored a major text on qualitative research methods. His Ph.D. is in sociology from Syracuse University.

Index